G000023137

The Long Road to Lavender Cottage

A Social History
by Victoria Seymour

First published in 2006
By Victoria Seymour

Copyright Victoria Seymour.

Email: mail@victoriaseymour.com
Website: www.victoriaseymour.com

ISBN: 0-9543901-4-8

Victoria Seymour has asserted her right to be identified as the author
of this work. No part of this publication may be produced,
transmitted or stored in a retrieval system in any form or by any
means without the written permission of the publishers.

A catalogue record for this book is available from the British Library.

Printed in Great Britain by

impression IT.
7, Moorhurst Road
St Leonards on Sea,
East Sussex
TN38 9NA

This book is dedicated, with profound thanks, to Wendy Johnson, without whose inspiration my writing career would not have begun.

My gratitude goes to those who recounted memories, comment and family and business details to this social history: Emily Crane. Mrs Carey. Mrs Enid Eldridge. Hazel Jones. Mrs Eunice Hance. Mr Jim Hoad, Miss Joyce Brewer. Ivor White. Noel Care. Brian Lawes. Roger Carey. Ewart Crane. Jonathan Milne. Diana Woolston. Eleanor Russell. Anonymous; Retired Hastings Borough Police Officer. Richard Pitcairn-Knowles. Wendy Johnson. Ray Gladwish. James Barnes-Phillips. Esther Carpenter. Jill Burrows. Tim Tidmarsh. Derek Burt. Christine Winter. Bill Moseley. Pat Held. George Ford. Holford Pitcher. Roger Tilbury. David Padgham. Angie Quinnell. Diane Funnell, June Turner. Leon Shepperdson. Peter Paine. Don Valentine. Vi Pratt. Daisy Jarman. Joan Head. Francis Cornwall. Rosemary Cruttenden. Hastings Borough Council Cemetery and Crematorium. Hastings and Rother Family History Society. Burslem Monumental Masons and their Hastings Branch Manager, Howard Whitelaw. Jo Turner and the Hastings Unitarian Church Records. John Turner and the St Helen's Methodist Church Records. William Marsh, Rev. Clive Lee, George Cornelius, Terry Hobbs, Wally Cornelius.

My thanks for use of images to Hastings Reference Library. Hastings and St Leonards Observer. Hounslow Local History Group. The British Library. Johnson Family Collection. Eunice Hance. Roger Carey. Pitcairn-Knowles Family Collection. Roger Tilbury. Brian Lawes Collection. Ken Brooks Collection. Tim White. Crane Family Collection. Ray Gladwish Collection. David Padgeham Collection. Tidmarsh Family Collection. Christine Winter Family Collection. Vi Pratt Family Collection. Daisy Jarman Family Collection. Ivor White, photographic enhancement. Additional photography, my son.

Every effort has been made to trace holders of copyrights. Any inadvertent omissions of acknowledgement or permission can be rectified in future editions.

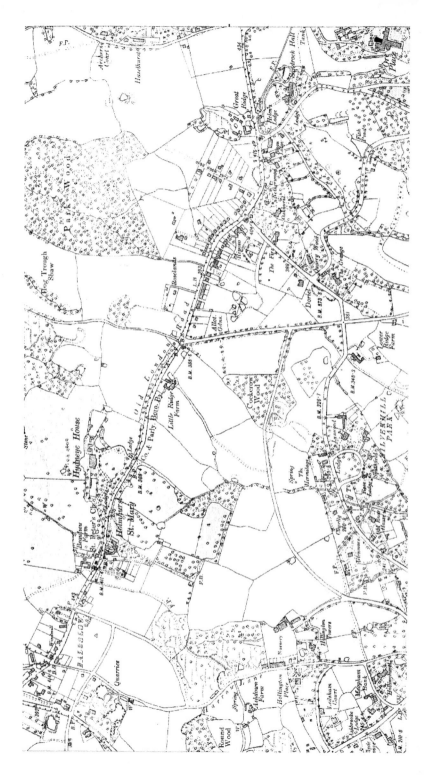

PART ONE.

EMILIE'S LIFE.

When Emilie Crane was born her parents were residing at Bessborough Gardens, near Vauxhall Bridge, London. The entry for their address in the 1871 census shows: Robert Crane, 39, foreman of engineers, born Shelford, Cambridgeshire and the other members of the household as Ellen Crane, aged 41, wife, born Scarborough Yorkshire, Mary Eleanor Crane, aged 16, born London, Robert Crane, aged nine, born London, Emilie Ethel Crane, aged one month, born Westminster. Also resident were Frederick William Kelsey, aged 31, boarder, unmarried, artist, deaf and dumb, born Horley Surrey and Edward Rosede Mullins, aged 22, lodger, unmarried, sculptor, born London.

The Victorian London into which Emilie was born was a place of cruel contrasts. New houses for the middle and upper classes stood not far from overcrowded slums, where people lived in appalling conditions. The population level of London surged during the 19th century, from about one million in 1800 to over 6 million one hundred years later. In 1848 the great Potato Famine struck Ireland and over 100,000 impoverished Irish fled their country and settled in London, making up almost 20% of the total population of the city. In 1873, an agricultural depression affected all sections of British farming and farmers were obliged to cut wages to their laborers, which added to the drift of the lower classes from the land towards the towns, increasing further to the impoverished masses of London. This population growth far exceeded London's ability to look after the basic needs of its citizens. Sanitary arrangements for the poor were inadequate to say the least and the universal use of coal-fired stoves created the health and life-threatening London fogs. However, there were social changes afoot that gradually led to the betterment of not only the poor in general but that of all women, who had very few rights.

Today, the terraced properties in Bessborough Gardens, with their well-preserved Victorian facades, are no longer family homes. As with so many of London's residential gardens and squares, the lower rooms are offices for businesses and organizations and the upper rooms are divided into apartments, some of which meet the high demand for accommodation for government and media staff, who make up a considerable part of the Westminster population.

Emilie Crane's position in the social class structure would have been of particular significance in her early years. She would have been perceived by Victorians as middle class: This level of the class structure was regarded as less socially acceptable than members of the upper middle class. Middle class children did not usually attend public (fee-paying) schools and the family had only one or two servants, as opposed to the many in higher class households. Middle class men were generally the owners of small businesses and shops or had jobs as lower-grade civil servants.

By looking at the period during which Emilie Crane grew from a child to an independent young woman and referring to her letters, it may be possible to define the influences that shaped her personality. Her kindness, generosity and sense of humour were probably innate but her surroundings and view of life could have given her sympathy for the plight of the lower classes and the lesser position of women in society. During her early years there were many government Acts that improved the lot of the poor and women. The period was also marked by the nascence of the Suffragette Movement. There was a flood of scientific and medical discoveries and inventions that would eventually change the course of ordinary people's lives.

Living in London as she did, it would have been easy for Emilie to attend concert-hall performances of the great music of her time; the composers Wagner, Brahms, Bizet, Strauss, Verdi, Tchaikovsky, Dvorak, Offenbach, Rimsky Korsakov, Caesar Frank, Debussy, Puccini, Gilbert and Sullivan, and Elgar were her contemporaries.
Reading was an important part of Emilie's life; Charles Dickens, a known favourite writer with her, died the year before she was born. Contemporary with Emilie were poets Browning, Tennyson, Stevenson, Rossetti, Kipling and Yeats. Also being published were

novelists Elliot, Sewell, Twain, Stevenson, Trollope, Sir Arthur Conan Doyle, Conrad and Wells. Dramas were being written by Ibsen, Chekhov, Yeats and Shaw. Coincidentally, Conrad lived at Bessborough Gardens in 1889 and the address is mentioned in his book Almayer's Folly.

By 1880, at the age of nine, Emilie Crane was a boarder at The Convent of St. Mary and St. Scholastica, The High Street, Feltham. Miss Mary Hilda Stewart was the Reverend Mother Superior. It is not known where Emilie's family was living at that time or why she went as a boarder. The community of nuns belonged to the Church of England and they lived the cloistered life under the rule of St. Benedict. The convent was governed by the mother and chapter of professed nuns, assisted by the advice of several priests. The institution earned an income from the sisters doing church embroidery and plain needlework and from the small orphanage and day school attached to the convent. Kelly's Directory 1880 listed 13 sisters in the convent, ranging in age from 23 to 51, most of them seamstresses and embroidresses, and one governess. There were 5 female boarders, Emilie being one of them. There was a 14 year old female domestic servant, and a 15 year old male domestic servant. There was also a visitor, noted as blind and deaf, whose occupation was knitter of woollen and cotton hosiery. The 1890 edition of Kelly's Middlesex directory had no entry for the convent so it's probable that the sisters had gone from Feltham by that time. There is a belief, supported by a note on a family tree that Emilie's older sister, Mary Eleanor became an Anglican nun. It seems it was contrary to the wishes and persuasion of her family. Mary Crane's name was not among the sisters at the Convent of St Mary and St Scholastica listed in the Kelly's Directory, thus dispelling the notion that Emilie was a pupil at the convent because her older sister was cloistered there. The strictures of life as a convent school boarder must have been difficult for Emilie; her mischievous sense of humour was probably developing by the age of nine. It appears that the needlework skills of the nuns made little impression on Emilie, as we know that she did not learn to knit until she was 63 and she had a dressmaker to make clothes for her in her latter years.

In an extract from a letter dated 1880 and written by Emilie's cousin, Pollie Chalk, we find that the young Emilie did not always go home for the entire school holidays. Whether this family visit was a treat or an emergency there is no indication.

"36, Devonshire Street,
Portland Place,
London.

We had Emilie staying with us last weekend and I took her home on Saturday and she returns back to school today, not to return home until Christmas, which time seems to come upon us very quickly"

It has been suggested that Emilie Crane had a connection with the Suffragettes but I have heard this theory propounded by a number of family researchers about women of this generation. I suspect it is sometimes a myth, created by an over-keen genealogist, in order to add colour to an otherwise uneventful life. However, instrumental in drawing up the Married Women's' Property Act in 1882 was Richard Pankhurst, whose wife, Emmeline Pankhurst, was the daughter of Robert Goulden and Sophia Crane. Emmeline's mother was a passionate feminist and started taking her daughter to women's suffrage (the right to vote) meetings in the early 1870s. Emmeline became the mother of Cristobel and Sylvia Pankhurst. So perhaps the name Crane in this political family tree generated the myth.

The first specimen we have of Emilie's handwriting is when she was nineteen, in a letter she sent from 6, Benfield Road, Clapham on the 6th June 1890. The letter is in connection with an unspecified newspaper cutting. Emilie' handwriting is bold and strong, no wilting violet this!

My Dear Aunt,
My father happened to see this in the Daily Telegraph this morning and thinking you might be interested in it, asked me to write and send it to you. He is very well but has no fresh news to tell you. My brother's little one has the measles, we fear, but we think it will be all right soon. It is a very pretty baby and being the first they are naturally anxious about it. We have had a great deal of excitement this week on account

4

*of the Derby. I suppose you have that in America as well. It is very
good fun but rather noisy. I hope my uncle and all my cousins are well.
With very much love from all.*
Believe me, (to be)
Your Affectionate Niece,
E. Ethel Crane

Emilie's brother, Robert Ewart Crane went to live in Guelph, Canada,
to take a job with the Bell Organ and Piano Company. The company
had a main branch office at 95 New Bond Street, London so probably
the contact was made there. Robert had already travelled extensively
in South America and spoke Spanish. The following letter reveals that
he was expecting a family visit from England but his plans for their
accommodation and his own domestic comfort had gone awry.

Guelph Ontario 12th October 1894

Dear Cousin Emily,

*I have been looking anxiously for any news of the "Labrador" but up
to the present have heard nothing of her whereabouts. They call her
an eight day boat, but you know what reliance is to be placed on
agents' yarns. She is not reported in this morning's paper. I do not
expect her to arrive in Quebec until tomorrow, and that would mean
Sunday in Montreal. They should be in time to catch the night train
from Montreal on Sunday evening, arriving in Toronto at 7 o'clock
Monday a.m. I shall go down to Toronto and in that event they should
reach here on Monday afternoon.*

*The way things have gone here caused us to be in a terrible muddle.
Father did not send my furniture off from England until just before he
sailed, so it will not get here for another fortnight or so. Meantime, we
have bought just the bare things necessary for our existence. I did not
know what to do with Father ~ it would cost them a great deal to go to
the Hotel until we got settled, so I bought another bedstead, and Emilie
will have to accommodate her self with the girl (nursemaid?) for the
time being. It is a pity it has happened like this, as it would have been*

5

so much nicer to have had the house all fixed ready for them, but it cannot be helped now.

Your affectionate cousin,
Rob

I imagine that Emilie, an unpretentious person, did not mind in the least being obliged to share a room with the nursemaid. In Letters from Lavender Cottage, Emilie's correspondence dated 27th January 1952, and sent to Marion and Beatrice, makes a reference to this voyage and a near-disaster that may explain the delay in the ship arriving, which her brother mentions:

"...Would Beatrice be good enough to let me have something about Labrador? I have been trying to describe the occasion when we were nearly wrecked by an iceberg but I can't remember whether Labrador was an asset in that case. I remember being tossed on the floor and a wailing passenger moaning at my side. I know it's a strange thing to ask but I want to write a description if I can..."

The 1901 census shows the 30 year-old Emilie Crane was living with her friend Clare Marriott at 10 Saltoun Road Brixton. The property was shared with Hermia L.Howes, a bookkeeper, aged 37; she was probably Emilie's cousin. In the street directory of 1901 the main occupant of 10 Saltoun Road is listed as J.Oates, who had accountancy qualifications. As this was a three storey house, with nine bedrooms we may assume that Emilie, Clare and Cousin Hermia were tenants or lodgers and as such they might not have been listed in a street directory. Perhaps Emilie came well recommended to Mr Oates because of her connection with her family of accountants. Number 45 Talma Road, Brixton, just around the corner from Saltoun Road, was the home of Emilie's parents, Robert and Ellen Crane. The census records Robert's employment as a domestic engineer. A collection of recently discovered postcards, sent to Canada from a family member travelling in England in 1907, shows that the visitor stayed with Robert Crane at 59 Kellett Road, Brixton, which is very close to Saltoun Road and Talma Road. Emilie's parents seemed to move house with unusual frequency for the times. At that period Brixton was undergoing a social change: Up until the Industrial Revolution and the coming of the railways, Brixton remained undeveloped and mainly agricultural. The first speculative development started after the construction of the Vauxhall Bridge in 1816. The small settlement underwent a huge transformation between the 1860s and 1890s, as railways and trams linked Brixton with the centre of London. In 1880, Brixton's Electric Avenue was so named, after it became the first street in the area to be lit by electricity. Large houses were constructed along the main trunk routes into Brixton, attracting the middle classes.

At the turn of the century Brixton underwent a social upheaval, as the middle classes gradually moved out, to be replaced by a huge working class population. Many of the big houses were converted into flats or boarding houses which proved very popular with theatre people working in the West End, thus creating the start of Brixton's close association with the arts. The photograph of Emilie, which was taken during her time at Brixton, shows a rather grim looking young woman, belying the personality that emerges in her letters. The stern expression is more probably a reflection of the photography style of the period. Smiling for a photograph was actively discouraged, except for children. For a man to been seen smiling in a photographic portrait was thought to convey an impression of a lightweight mind and even women were advised merely to look pleasant. There is no date for Emilie's commencement of employment but it is known that in 1918 she was secretary and/or departmental manager at J & J Paton, an Education Agency in Paternoster Square. The purpose of an Education Agent a hundred years ago is only a little different from that of today. In the past, British parents, especially those living overseas, would use an education agency to recommend a list of boarding schools suitable for their children. These days it is more likely to be foreign parents who are looking for a British education or a short term, residential school for English language tuition, who use the services of an education agency.

While working at the agency, Emilie introduced her niece, Olive Crane, daughter of her brother Robert, to a self-educated and much loved man, George Henry Sutherland, they eventually married. It is said that Emilie encouraged George's self-education; he was killed in the First World War. It is interesting that the first offices of Crane,

Houghton & Crane, Accountants, were also in Paternoster Row. In WWII the district was attacked with thousands of incendiary bombs during the night of 29th/30th December 1940. A vast area surrounding St Paul's Cathedral was consumed by the firestorm that followed the raid and the accountancy and education agency offices were destroyed. Olive Crane's granddaughter, Diana Woolston of Hayes, close to Bromley, in Kent, has affectionate recollections of all her great aunts, among whom Emilie was numbered. She said that they were enthusiastic bridge players and when young some of them had motor bikes. They had a cigarette machine installed in the hall of their house at 104 Croydon Road, Anerley, London, where they all lived together; Emilie smoked all her life. Diana said of the great-aunts: 'They were a great bunch - girls about town'. She also remembered that towards the end of her life, Emilie gave Diana a two-and-sixpenny piece and her younger sister one penny. The coins were of a similar size and Emilie's failing eyesight could not detect the difference between them. Diana Woolston contributed the copy of a page from a family autograph book, undated, that shows a pencil and watercolour drawing by Emilie Crane. It is possible that she composed the little verse herself, bearing in mind similar lines she wrote about her garden in the 1950s. The autograph reads: 'Who does not recollect the hours, when burning words and phrases, were lavished on these shining flowers, "Buttercups and Daisies"' The drawing and script suggest an immature hand so we may presume it is a youthful effort.

By 1913, when Emilie was in her forties, she was travelling abroad in a way that was unusual among the female members of her class. She was no doubt enabled by her single state and encouraged by her circle of 'racy' companions. We learn in the quote from a letter, written by Emilie's father that her life-long friend, Miss Clare Marriott was already well established in Emilie's life by this time:

Emilie's father, Robert Crane, wrote on 12th August 1913, from 88, Maple Road, Penge to his niece, Mrs Emily King, nee Howes, living in Ontario:

"...Our "Em" has been away for her holiday on the Continent, to Heidelberg, Cologne and Brussels and I think trying to do some business for her firm at the same time. She returns at the end of this week with her much-attached friend Miss Marriott..."

Can one sense a hint of disapproval of Miss Marriott in her father's reference to Emilie's friend?

On the 15th August 1916 Emilie's father wrote to his niece Emily King, (Wendy Johnson's great grandmother) of Ontario, from his home at Maple Road. In the letter we learn that Emilie was in Norway.

"Emilie and her friends are in Norway. I had a letter from her this morning. They had a very rough journey. They stayed a few days at Bergen and are off further north partly round the coast and up the fiords and partly inland. It would be a way too rough for one (me). I cannot help feeling that after her very long hours at work for many weeks, she would have been better for a more restful change. However in these matters one must consider oneself fortunate if allowed to express an opinion."

It seems extraordinary that at a time when one of the most terrible battles of WWI was raging Emilie should undertake a pleasure sea voyage. Perhaps it only seems shocking in retrospect.   On 1st July 1916 at 7.30am, 11 British divisions (100,000 men) went 'over the top' towards the Germans. By 9.00am 22,000 were dead and another 40,000 were wounded in what became known as the Battle of the Somme, which raged for another five months, with over one million British men, wounded and slaughtered. Although the war at sea in WWI did not reach the ferocity of that of WWII one marvels at Emilie's courage or perhaps, fool-hardiness in making the trip. Mr Crane's closing comments also give further insight into Emilie's nature and that she was not to be swayed by the criticism or advice of her father.

By 1927, when we may presume Emilie was approaching retirement, if not already retired, her father was living at 123, Croydon Road, Anerley, London. On May 31st he wrote to his niece Emily Crane, to insist that on his death she should receive a pocket watch, which was a family heirloom, from the days when the Cranes were, to quote Emilie, 'more illustrious'.

He wrote:
"I know if I passed away suddenly the watch would not be sent to you and, as I know no one who has been one hundredth part so good to me

as you have, I felt I was doing a truly just and worthy thing, since no other member of my family, not even my Emilie, was entitled to it".

Emilie's father died a few months later, aged 97.

It does seem that there was indeed a time when the Cranes were more illustrious. In a previously unpublished letter sent to her Cousin Marion Ellis about their family tree Emilie said:

"Some time in the 1890s my father and brother (both called Robert), ambitious to know their ancestry, wrote to the Herald's College, the institution which provides genealogies at a price. They received a kind of chart giving what details could be found. Way back, I don't know when, there seems to have been a Sir Robert Crane whose tomb is or was in a Suffolk churchyard. (It emerged later that Sir Robert died in 1642 and the tomb is Chiltern, in Suffolk). When and where he was knighted history did not relate but I gleaned he was not a Crusader, his legs not being crossed, therefore he did not date from those times. The crest on the stone was, "on a wreath or and gules crane passant, ppr; beaked or". I do not know the heraldic meaning of the ppr here.

Sir Robert now disappears from the scene but very much later, near Crishall, appears a Crane family, Robert Crane and his wife (Emilie's grandparents) and their sons, Robert, William and Thomas and daughters Emma (Aunt Ward) Mary and another, name unknown. My father, Robert also named his son Robert and I feel annoyed with my nephew because he has broken the chain and not used the name for any of his sons. My grandmother's maiden name was Dellow, possibly of French origin. Emma Crane (Wendy Johnson's great-great grandmother) married Mr Howes and departed to find fortune in Canada. Mary Crane married Mr Chalk, manager of a railway firm in Oxford Street, they were Pollie's parents. William vanished, I never met him. Thomas was a very genial man but it is said he drank too much, he also disappeared. I think there was Henry but he became mentally afflicted as the result of an accident. The other un-named daughter married Ralph Bigland, son of Sir Ralph Bigland and she was lady-in-waiting to three sovereigns. Sir Ralph bequeathed a sum of money to my father and his brothers but Ralph was a spendthrift and made a deed of gift by which a lawyer obtained this money; why a deed of gift should supersede a will I don't know. Poor Aunt Bigland died in a kind of home for gentlewomen in Hampton Court. There was a Mrs Corby who lived with Grandmother Emma after she was widowed, they may have been sisters. There were some Drages but I don't know what relation they were, but they did refer to Mrs Corby as "Aunt"; I was very young at the time. I presume that those who did not leave Crishall are buried in the churchyard there but I did not see the graves as we rarely went there. There is no fear the Cranes will die out as my nephew Robert has four healthy lads as well as two daughters. I only have news of the family from my nieces, the boys just send Christmas cards. My great nephew, Emily's boy, is very good; he made me a genealogical tree dating from my father and I was appalled at the number of descendants, not all Crane of course".

While not wishing to digress from Emilie's personal story with too much genealogical detail, it may be helpful to understand how it came about that she had relatives, including the generous Cousin Marion Ellis, living in Canada. Emilie's ancestor, the former Miss Emma Crane, later Mrs M. George Howes, went to live in Mimico, Ontario in 1854, with her husband and their three young daughters. Two of the girls died in a scarlet fever outbreak and one of twin infant boys died in 1855, the same year Emma's husband also died. Emma's surviving daughter, Emily Marion had been born in London, England in 1847; her daughter, Ethel Emily was Marion's mother, she also had another daughter, Eleanor, who is Wendy Johnson's mother. Marion was interested in family history and very careful about keeping documents and letters and she also wrote an extensive diary. She worked in the tax department so no doubt an orderly attitude to paperwork came naturally to her. Cousin Marion set up home with Miss Beatrice Taylor, who was the women's page editor of the London Free Press in Ontario, a theatre critic and a published poet. Beatrice also wrote a series of pieces for the LFP under the pseudonym Tireless Traveller, reporting on excursions made in the rural areas of southwestern Ontario, accompanied by Marion, who was dubbed The Explorer, for the purposes of the article. In her letters to Marion, Emilie made several references to Beatrice's newspaper articles, suggesting she should write a book, so Emilie must have seen the pieces. Beatrice's writing is lyrical and full of affection for the people they met and descriptions of the buildings, plants and scenery they saw; no wonder Emilie enjoyed the articles so much. Certainly, if Emilie Crane and her friend Clare Marriot had lived near to Marion and Beatrice the four women would have been friends, as they seemed to share similar interests. For the greater time that that Emilie was writing to Marion and Beatrice they lived at 138, Broughdale Avenue, London, Ontario.

For the year 1928 there is another address for Emilie, which was no doubt also the home of her friend Clare Marriott; 93, Kings Court Road, Streatham. S W. Included with this information was a note of another address, 143 Cannon Street, which I suspected was the address of Emilie's employment. Researching the records for that period showed that 143 Cannon Street housed the offices of around 13 businesses of an astonishing variety of titles, including; heating engineers, export and importers, insurance claim assessors, travelling rug merchants, solicitors, surveyors and there, at the end of the list, J&J Paton, Educational Agents. 143 Cannon Street is now a McDonald's outlet. So it seems that Emilie remained with the same firm until the date of her retirement and her departure to Hastings, which followed soon after. I am sometimes asked if there is any known reason why Emilie Crane did not marry. Possibly an explanation can be found in Victorian history: Attendance at Elementary Schools was made compulsory in 1871 and London University opened all degrees to women. It seems unlikely that Emilie Crane attended university but it can be presumed from her subsequent employment she underwent some kind of secretarial training. Prior to 1871, young girls had already started to attend school to learn reading, writing, and arithmetic. Older girls studied books that instructed them in the manners of society and the running of the home, to prepare for marriage. Victorian society valued the ideal of the perfect woman and set strict standards for the lives of women of the middle and upper classes for their role of wife and mother. However, in most respects, women often did not benefit from matrimony, as on marrying they relinquished their rights with reference to money and property. Once married, women's status depended upon that of their husband. Victorian society never let women forget family was its cornerstone and a woman's sole function marriage and procreation. Women who questioned these ideals were regarded as a threat to the fabric of society. Yet biology colluded against marriage as a goal for all women, as throughout the greater part of the Victorian era there was a significant population imbalance of the sexes, which inevitably condemned many women to the role of spinster. Victorian society did not accord these single women the same respect as married women; believing that a woman without a husband was worthless.

If they had no family to support them, many unmarried, middle-class women found themselves in a difficult financial position and were obliged to earn their own living. Others sought employment partly in response to Victorian attitudes that disapproved of idleness. From the mid-century, educated women began to enter certain professional and clerical occupations. But these women were often up against the prejudice created by the social values of the times and the Victorian myth of the ideal woman. But not all Victorian spinsters regarded their lives as unfortunate. Some women and I believe Emilie Crane to be one of these, saw gainful employment as a preferable alternative to marriage, not a poor substitute. In spite of considerable legislation to improve the lot of married women during the 19th century and a later relaxation of strict Victorian social attitudes, by the time Emilie was of marriageable age the role of a wife may not have been very appealing to her. She would have had to set aside personal ambition and her own interests, to meet the Victorian ideal of a wife; she would probably have been expected to bear many children and risk her health in the process. Not once in her letters did she express any regret at not having been married. She took an interest in the younger members of her family but did not complain about having no children of her own. Perhaps Emilie Crane just did not find men attractive. That is not to say that her preference was for women. Her sharing of home with other women was probably for economic and companionship reasons and the arrangement was very common among her generation. Can Emilie's view of the opposite sex be divined from the words in a play that she wrote, which was published in The Boys Own Paper when she was fifty? The character of a maiden aunt is scolding an impertinent office boy, who refers to her as "sir". She says: "To be likened to a nasty, dirty smoky man! Men! Why, I wouldn't touch the best of them with a red hot poker! Thank goodness I never had anything to do with men!

Emilie and Clare arrived at Hastings in 1929 and at first they shared a home called Wayside in Westfield Lane, close to Baldslow Village,

13

which is situated on the Ridge and within reasonable walking distance of Lavender Cottage, where their friend, Miss Edith Lake, lived with her elderly mother. The style of architecture of Lavender Cottage appears to be 1920s; prior to its occupation by Emilie Crane and her friends A. G Seward was the first resident named at the address. In 1932 the Hastings street directory's listing changed the occupant of Lavender Cottage to Miss Lake, after the death of her mother. In a letter to Marion and Beatrice, dated December 27th 1947 we are given an explanation of how Emilie and her friend Clare Marriott eventually came to live in Lavender Cottage. After detailed thanks for the food parcels from Canada Emilie writes:

" When I left the office, where I was managing a department for a Scholastic Agency after WWI, Edith Lake, a friend living at Sutton, came down to Hastings with her mother and was anxious for us to make our home here also. She bought us a bungalow, which I think you saw, where we had quite a nice home. When her mother died, Edith wanted to come and live with us but the bungalow was too small so she sold it and between us we bought this house. Later she returned us the money we had paid, to avoid difficulties if anything happened to her.

So now we pay her a modest rent, as she is very kind. I forgot to say that she built on to this house as it was also too small. Things are alright as long as EL keeps well but her head is very bad, she cannot remember anything and the doctor says her brain arteries are hardening. It will be a bad day when she goes but I expect something will turn up, it always does".

The Hastings and St Leonards in the 1930s was a town of clear social and financial divisions. The town's main sources of income were visitors and to a lesser extent, the fishing fleet. The upper-end of the income scale was represented by hoteliers, the owners of guest and boarding houses, convalescent homes and residential school and the trades that served them, as well as the moneyed occupants of the large houses in and around the town. Within the lower social orders and the fishing community very real poverty existed. The local fishermen were not only at the mercy of the elements when earning their living but the industry had been in decline since the 1920s. In the 1930s many fishermen gave up going to sea and took employment in the building trade or with Hastings Corporation and the gas and electric works. The fishermen's wives traditionally found various means to bring in money: They boarded summer visitors, took in washing, sold fish or did shop work. Even the children of the fishermen's families were expected to add to the family revenue, delivering fish orders or helping with child-minding. In the early 1930s, Hastings and St Leonards began to experience what was hailed as a renaissance, under a scheme first devised by a town planner Doctor Thomas Adams and carried forward by the Borough Engineer, Sidney Little. He earned himself the nick-name 'The Concrete King' due to his evident fondness for the building material. During his 'reign' many modernisation schemes took shape, thus providing some, but not enough, work for local fishermen and the unemployed of the town. Sidney Little masterminded the complete rebuilding of the seafront between Marine Parade and the Marina, the modernisation of the White Rock Baths, the building of the St Leonards Bathing Pool, in its time one of the biggest in Europe and the construction of possibly the world's first underground car park. This structure, along with a covered promenade, called Bottle Alley, because of its broken glass murals, was incorporated in the seafront development. Behind these apparent improvements to the town there was a harsher story. Hastings and St Leonards, like the rest of the country, was suffering the effects of the Great Depression, brought about by the economic pressures resulting from the Great War and the world-wide financial decline that developed in the aftermath. In 1933 Hastings and St Leonards had 2,000 unemployed. In the first week of January of that year, from the £25 collected at a Christmas carol concert, given by the Wellington Square Boys Band, 1,600 food parcels were provided to the unemployed. The money was sufficient to buy 2 tons of sprouts, 450 cabbages, a quarter of a ton each of onions and carrots and 425 loaves. The Hastings and St Leonards Observer reported: 'Men of all types and ages went away carrying parcels, knowing that a good meal awaited them and the hungry little mouths at home'. Hastings' Mayor addressed an appeal to all classes: 'In other towns it has been found that the working classes are ready to aid those who are unemployed by contributing a small, weekly sum to help with the expenses of finding work. I hope that this feeling will find expression in Hastings and St Leonards' people of all other classes and prompt them to send as much as they can afford'. The mayor also introduced a scheme to provide casual labour to the unemployed. He invited householders who had small maintenance tasks about their homes in need of attention to contact him and he would pass on details of the work to the men, who could be found at the recreation centre for the unemployed, which had been set up in the old post office. The local newspaper ran a full-page advertising promotion, sponsored by local building and maintenance firms, under the banner, 'Give Work to Make Work; trained and skilled workers are now condemned to enforced idleness-fight the unemployment demon!'

A letter writer to the Observer came up with a novel solution to the 'idleness'; viewed with today's values the idea seems insulting and patronising. The letter began with the perennial complaint about the pavement nuisance created by dogs. It went on to suggest that a reward of five shillings (25p) could be paid to anyone who witnessed and reported the animal's owner to the police for the offence of allowing a dog to foul the pavement. The writer pointed out that the act of finding culprits and helping to bring about a conviction could provide a source of occupation and cash to the unemployed.   In early January 1933, the excavation of the beach to construct the Hastings Old Town boating lake began and it gave work to 60 men. These men worked part-time, turn and turn about, in order to give a wage to as many of the unemployed as possible. It proved to be a winter of bitter cold and many of the poorest in the town had inadequate clothing. A clothing and aid office was operating from 49, Cambridge Gardens and in the first weeks of January they provided boots and bedding as well as 3,322 garments to 230 men, 120 women and 257 children. The office issued a warning that the call for yet more clothing would continue for some time to come. In mid-February the men's clothing section had to be closed as it had run out of supplies. The various unemployment benefits and allowances of the day were sufficient only for the barest essentials and supplies of cold weather clothing were not among these. There were various other bodies at work to relieve the privations of the poor. Since 1914 a charitable boot and clothing fund, administered by the Hastings Chief of Police and his force, had aided the poorest in the town. A report in 1932 said that in the previous year the fund had: 'Provided 341 pairs of boots and shoes, 658 pairs of stockings and socks and 105 other garments, together with quantities of beef, bread and potatoes, coal and groceries". The total amount spent by the fund for that year was £210. In March 1933 Lord Eustace Percy, the town's Conservative MP addressed a meeting on the subject of the depression at the Queen's Hotel in Hastings: 'We are living in the most dangerous and difficult era since the fall of the Roman Empire. We have grave problems to face and we may have to throw overboard more prejudices than did our fathers'. He predicted the possible end of European civilization. Portentous words! The conditions of hardship inflicted on the working classes by the depression prevailed in some measure up until the start of WWII. It certainly affected my family; meals consisting of just mashed potato and fried onions were a common dish at our table, sometimes with the 'luxury' addition of a white sauce made from milk and flour. We never had any new things and we were grateful for occasional hand-me-downs of clothing or domestic chattels from our betters. No wonder that many people in the lower classes were already well trained for the shortages of WWII or thought that things were actually better under rationing.

The economic situation of the times is highlighted in Emilie's remark about 'knitting for the unemployed', in a letter that she wrote from Lavender Cottage to her cousin Ethel in Canada on 10th February 1934. After enquiring and commenting on Ethel's family health concerns, Emilie turns to matters at home:

"...I wonder what kind of winter you have had or are still having. We read terrible accounts of snow in New York and I suppose it is much the same in Canada. It has been pretty bad here, though we have had only two slight snow falls in Hastings but the wind has been bitter and it has taken a good deal of time to keep the birds alive with food and water. Otherwise we have been brisk in making garments for the unemployed here and I have actually learned to knit! I fear I looked upon that occupation very scornfully before, as being suitable only for old ladies who wore caps. But owing to the fact that I suddenly found I was an old lady myself (minus the cap though) I have quite taken to it and have achieved quite a number of jumpers during the past few months. This feat was attended by so many S.O.S.s, when stitches went astray or mysteriously multiplied themselves that my friends do not regard my new undertaking as an unmixed blessing. Still, it is as well to do something useful and one gets through a lot while listening to the

wireless, which was presented to my friend by a brother and is a great joy to us. We get some good lectures and follow the French, German and Spanish lessons quite industriously. I went London just before Christmas to see Louise and the children. They wished me to go for Christmas but my nerves are not right yet, so I though it best to avoid travelling at that time.....
Yours affectionately,

Emilie".

Although retired Emilie did not spend all her time knitting and listening to the radio: She was a busy member of her church, as I learned from documents, discovered after the publication of Letters from Lavender Cottage She was a member of the Unitarian Free Christian Church for many years. But as her letters from her residence on the Ridge referred to her attending a 'nice little church' I had wrongly presumed that she worshipped at St Peters Church on the Ridge. (The confusion during my research was compounded by Emilie's remarks about being cared for during her illness by a Mrs Cole from her church; both St Peter's and the Unitarian Free Christian Church in Hastings, Emilie's actual church, had active members called Mrs Cole). I had supposed too, that as Emilie was attached to things traditional, that the Anglican Church would have been her place of her worship. However, Unitarianism must have been in the family for some time. A cutting from 'Christian Life' dated 16th September 1899, preserved by the grandson of Emilie's brother, Robert Ewart Crane, says,

'At Southend-on-Sea ... A congregation of encouraging dimensions met at the Unitarian Chapel on Sunday evening, to listen to the special discourse on "Death" delivered by Mr R. Ewart Crane...'

So, some of the family at least had been of the Unitarian persuasion. I knew nothing of the fundamentals of Unitarianism but their website provided a 21st century analysis of their beliefs. 'Unitarians believe that everyone has the right to seek truth and meaning for themselves and that the fundamental tools for doing this are your own life experience, your reflection upon it, your intuitive understanding and the promptings of your own conscience. The best setting for this is a community that welcomes you for who you are, complete with your beliefs, doubts and questions. The Unitarians say: "We can be called religious liberal; religious because we unite to celebrate and affirm values that embrace and reflect a greater reality than self; liberal because we claim no exclusive revelation or status for ourselves; because we afford respect and toleration to those who follow different paths of faith. We are called 'Unitarians' because of our traditional insistence on divine unity, the oneness of God and because we affirm the essential unity of humankind and of creation.'

From Emilie's letters we can gather that she was something of a free thinker, who might have been ill at ease with rigid religious tenets or rules of an unreasonable kind. Even in her declining months, when her mental and physical health were failing her, she wrote as much, in a letter sent from what we would now call a care home, in Laton Road, Hastings, to which she had hastily removed herself from Lavender Cottage. (In her confusion she thought it was a guest house).

...13th April 1955...

"...I have not any cheerful news to give you and am very sorry to communicate anything which is not lively but I feel I must write.

My move from Lavender Cottage was somewhat stormy; the good lady and myself disagreed and I went hurriedly, finding refuge here and removing all my furniture before realising that I had struck a guest house, where you are under supervision and do not go your own way! As I did not agree with the various orders the inhabitants are not very fond of me and my limits are somewhat irritating. I must confess I was not over agreeable and find myself rather fed up with rules! Please excuse my writing, I have no proper pen and cannot go out to buy minus an escort...I was interrupted by the head lady entering, so had to make polite remarks. But will write more. She is not a bad old thing but I can't stand being 'tied up'...

Emilie's reference to being 'tied up' does not mean physical restraint, as one horrified reader of Letters from Lavender Cottage assumed, but 'tied down' as in constrained by rules. There is a Crane Family legend that Emile attempted an escape from this residence by climbing out of a window and down a drainpipe. One might doubt her ability to

Bressington Gardens. Emilie Crane's birthplace

Convent of St Mary and Scholastica, Feltham

10, Saltoun Road.
Emilie's home in 1901

Emilie's father,
Robert Ewart Crane

Emilie's brother, Robert
Ewart Crane

Emilie Crane aged 30

Emilie's sister in-law and family, about 1894. The baby on the nursemaid's lap is a third Robert Ewart Crane, Emilie's nephew.

Emilie (third from right) at the wedding of her niece Sybil Milne (nee Crane) 1928

Lavender Cottage,
The Ridge,
Hastings
Feb 10/1934

My dear Ethel,

It was very kind of you to write and
tell me how Cousin Emily was, as your time must
indeed be occupied. I am so sorry she does not
improve - it is a terrible ordeal for anyone of such
splendid activity to be forced into inaction like this.
I know, however, how courageous she is, and will not
give way, even under such a trial. But it needs
great fortitude to sustain it. What an amount of
work it must make for you and Emma, running
a house in such an anxious time. I wonder what
kind of winter you have had, or are still having?
We read terrible accounts of snow in New York,
and I suppose it is much the same in Canada.
It has been pretty bad here, though we have had
only two slight snowfalls in Hastings, but the
wind has been bitter, and it has taken a good
deal of time to keep the birds alive with food &
water. Otherwise, we have been brisk in making
garments for the unemployed here, and I have
actually learnt to knit! I fear I looked upon
that occupation very scornfully heretofore, as being
suitable only for old ladies who wore caps, but,
possibly owing to the fact that I suddenly found
I was an old lady myself (minus the cap, though)
I have quite taken to it, and have achieved
quite a number of jumpers during the past

Emilie's first known letter
from Lavender Cottage.

24

The Unitarian Church, Emilie's place of worship in Hastings

Lavender Cottage 1950

Emilie, aged 79, seated on the steps of
Lavender Cottage

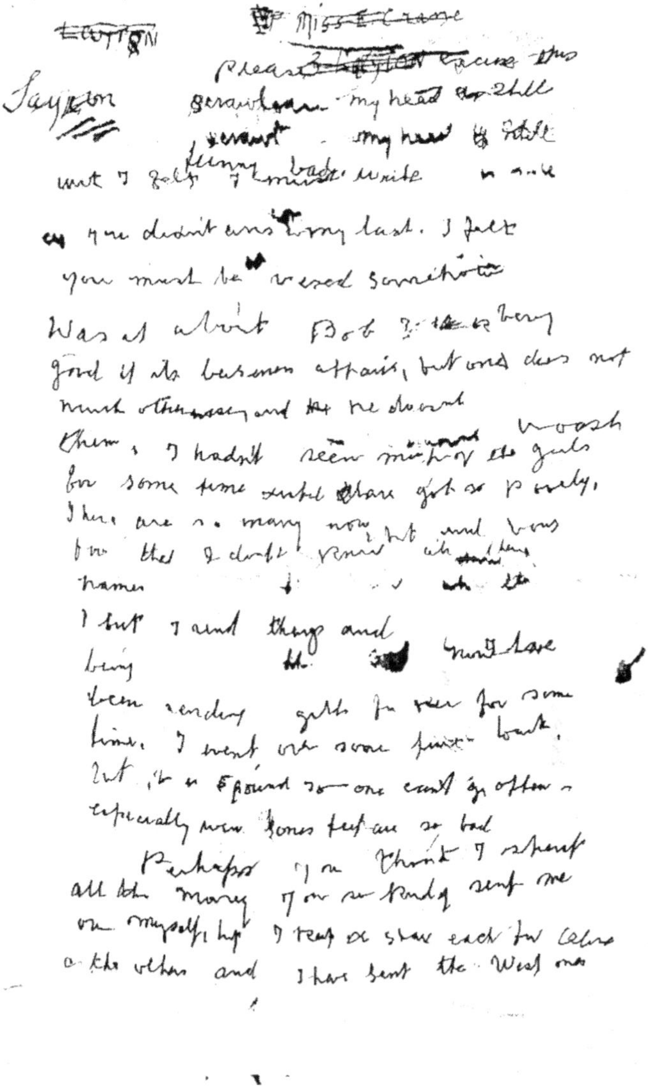
~~Miss Crowe~~

Please excuse this scrawl — my head is still feeling bad but I felt I must write as you didn't answer my last. I felt you must be vexed somehow. Was it about Bob? [illegible] very good if its business affairs, but one does not mind otherwise and he doesn't [illegible] them. I hadn't seen much of the girls for some time until [illegible] got so poorly. There are so many now [illegible] and boys [illegible] that I don't remember [illegible] names [illegible]

[illegible] must have been sending gifts [illegible] for some time. I went over some time back. but it is a pound so one can't go often — especially now [illegible] feet are so bad

Perhaps you think I spent all the money you so kindly sent me on myself, but I kept a share each for Celia & the others and I have sent the West ones

Emilie's last letter
written in May 1955

Emilie's 21st Century relative, Emily Crane, American Citizen, aged 14, 2004

28

accomplish this, being frail and aged 85 but I cherish the image. Yet she was certainly spirited; at aged 76, in January 1947, Emilie wrote in a letter of a walking misadventure, which reveals her feisty nature,

..."*We have had sharp frosts and the snow round our special part has kept us indoors for some time, as the corporation does nothing for the roads here. I had a few days in bed just before Christmas. I went to see an old lady in a nursing home; walking home I took a short cut through the woods and fell into a two-foot deep bog. I got soaking wet and nearly ruined my dress and coat. However, a kind neighbour repaired them so no harm was done except for myself suffering slight shock...*"

In 2005 Wendy Johnson's mother, Eleanor Russell, moved from her flat in London Ontario to a care residence near her daughter and son-in-law's home in Mississauga. The move necessitated a sorting and disposal of possessions and among old papers Wendy found an interesting item. She emailed me: 'I have been going through a box of things I brought back from Mom's. In a tiny 1930 diary written by Emma King, my grandmother's sister, is this':

"Arrived at St. Leonards on the Sea about dinner time. Stayed at The Royal Victoria Hotel. Left St. Leonards on July 12th after lunch. Spent the a.m. driving around. Drove to Valdelo and saw Emily Crane and had afternoon tea with her".

Wendy had previously given me, from her family keepsakes, an unused, vintage postcard from the Victoria Hotel at St Leonards; it is the sort of stationery that would have been available for the use of guests. After the discovery of the diary the presence of the hotel postcard among old papers fell into place. Wendy also found the photo album from that trip but there is neither mention of Emilie nor any suggestion of what Valdelo might be; the name of a house, tea rooms, who can say?

The previous year Emma's mother must have come to Hastings because she sent her daughter a short note, accompanied by a newspaper clipping. The note said:

Dear Emma, July 23rd.
Enclosed diagram of the storm and where it was worst. A good thing

we were not in London. We like it here-don't know where we go
next...Love to you all, Mother.

The storm to which the note referred had happened on Saturday afternoon, July 22nd 1929. London had been at the centre of the storm but the southeast and eastern coasts also suffered severely and a woman in a fishing boat was drowned at Hastings. The newspaper clipping from an unknown, national daily read; '
"Mrs Lillian Pollard of Woking, Surrey was the victim of a wave, which dashed up the beach at Hastings. It swept over the boat in which she had been on a fishing expedition with her husband, a friend and 'Jumbo' White, a boatman. Boats dashed to the rescue and the men were revived. Mr White said: "I was rowing towards the shore with the sea as smooth as a plate. Halfway through the harbour at about 100 yards from the shore I saw a wave about 20 feet high. We could not avoid it. I turned the boat end-on but the wave hit us and over we went. I have never seen anything like it before. The rebound from the shore was worse than the actual wave." Mr Wilkins, an official from Hastings Pier Company said to the newspaper that it had suddenly become dark and beyond the pier he saw what looked like a white wall on the water. It dashed up the beach at great speed and in a couple of minutes or so it had spent itself".

On learning that Emilie Crane had worshipped at what is now called the Unitarian Church in South Terrace, Hastings, I hoped that there might still be some record of her attendance, so I approached the contact named in our local Citizens Guide. I was touched by the warm response from church member by Mrs Jo Turner and her willingness to help my research.
The Unitarian Church frontage is set flush within a row of modest Victorian houses, which has a pub at either end. On entering the church I was keenly aware that I was viewing the interior of a building much loved and frequented by Emilie Crane and her two friends, Clare Marriot and Edith Lake. I grew up in the High Anglican Church and became accustomed to its statues and gilded ornamentation, so I was struck by the comparative absence of religious artifacts, except for a stained glass window in the porch, depicting a flame above a chalice, the symbol of Unitarianism. Facing the entrance is a speaker's podium; opposite to this is the gallery, where the Church Literary Society held

its weekly meetings in Emilie's days. Mrs Turner had taken considerable trouble in hunting for the church records between 1930 and 1955, as well as material on the establishment of the faith in Hastings. On an April afternoon two weeks later I sat alone in the gallery, perusing old minute books and committee notes, while a sewing party of church ladies tinkled teacups, as they chatted and worked in the main body of the church; the sound was pleasant and comforting, it must have been just like that in Emilie's times.

The first reference to Unitarianism in Hastings goes back to 1819-20, when a Mr Richard Wright toured the area on behalf of the London Unitarian Christian Society. He wrote in 1821 that he could find no place to preach, other than a room used by Methodists, who threatened to abandon the accommodation if it was used by the Unitarians. According to veteran, local newspaper reporter, Francis Cornwall, over one hundred years later this underlying hostility between the different religious factions still prevailed and the Nonconformists in the town must have been a prime target for disapproval.   In March 1860, a group of notable Hastings Unitarians hired a room in the town centre Music Hall, later called the Public Hall, (now Yates Wine Bar), for a service given before a congregation of twelve worshipers. After four weeks the proprietor of the hall refused further gatherings, so the Unitarians hired the Market Room of the Swan Hotel, in Old Town Hastings, which they used for seven years. The congregation collected money to build their own church and after nine years, for the sum of £254, they purchased a plot that was part of the Great Brook Estate, known today as South Terrace but at that time the land was pasture and water meadows, where children gathered watercress; the land was farmed by dairyman Daniel Murdock. The cornerstone of the church was laid on Wednesday, 2nd October 1867, followed by a tea at the Castle Hotel. The new church building was in the Roman Doric style, with a gallery that increased the seating capacity to 250. Over its early years the church was attended by many prominent people visiting the town, along with well known local residents, including the first female medical doctor, Elisabeth Blackwell. The Hastings Unitarian Church is now overlooked by the Priory Meadow Shopping Centre, built on the Central Cricket Ground, and crowded in by buildings on all sides.
In a booklet to mark the centenary of the Unitarian Free Christian Church, by the Rev. Denbigh Hilton, I discovered the hoped-for

references to Emilie and her friends: "Among the much loved members of the church in the thirties were Miss. C. Marriott, Miss. E. Crane and Miss. E. Lake. These three were affectionately known as the "Lavender Ladies" (the name of their cottage). The three friends gave many memorable garden parties and all held various offices in the church and on the Postal Mission. Miss Marriott's niece was Miss Kathleen Witcombe of Hurst Green, who endeared herself to the fellowship by her personality and nature talks at our Women's League. She and her father attended our services whenever they could." Rev Hilton mentions the various people who travelled some distance to the church, including: "...the "Lavender Ladies" from the Ridge, who in their declining years, though of modest means, felt it very much worth their while to come to services by taxi on every possible occasion". Mrs Jo Turner remembers the late Rev: Hilton well as, 'a Lancashire man, who retained his strong northern accent but it was rounded and very warm and a delight to listen to. His wife Muriel wrote several books of poems and reflective writings". Mrs Turner provided me with a collection of old minute books and papers for the years 1929 to the late 1950s, which proved to be a rewarding source of material on Emilie and her friends.

In the minutes of the AGM of the church dated 12th February 1931; the report closes with a welcome to five members who have joined in the past year; The Misses Florence, Elsie Davis, Miss Crane, Miss Marriott and Mrs Child. It was also noted that Edith Lake's mother died in January 1931.

From AGM for 1932: On 23rd July 1931. 'Miss Lake kindly lent her home for an American Tea and Whist Drive. The proceeds were £3'. I presume the tea was a Ridge version of America's rural get-togethers, when every guest brought a supply of food.

In loose-leaf papers; possibly rough notes for the meeting minutes, I found:

'On 13th July 1934 a social was held at Lavender Cottage by the kind invitation of Miss Lake, to welcome our new minister. It was an enjoyable occasion and about 40 guests were present including Miss Muriel Byers, (the minister's fiancée)'.

The minister of the Unitarian Free Christian Church, Denbigh Hilton, who is mentioned as 'our minister' several times in Emilie's letters, joined the church in 1934. It was he and his wife who started the Literary and Discussion Society that met fortnightly during the winter months. On 13th September 1934 Mr Denbigh Hilton married Miss Muriel Byers at Croydon. The Hon Sec had "the privilege and pleasure of being a guest at this delightful function". The usual summer outing did not take place that year as it was unanimously agreed at the congregational meeting on 10th June 1934 that the price of the outing tickets should go towards defraying the debt to the builders, who had carried out repairs to the church.

From church minutes 1934: "As a result of continued illness, the Treasurer of the Church, Miss Cheshire has been obliged to resign. This is difficult and special work and we are most fortunate in securing Miss Clare Marriot, who has consented to fill this office". We know from Emilie's comments in her letters that Clare was a stickler for accuracy in her household accounts and under Clare's guidance the church finances flourished and by 1936 it became possible to open an emergency fund for the upkeep of the building.

Notes for AGM 1935

On June 29th the Misses Lake, Marriott and Crane held an American Tea and a garden party at Lavender Cottage, to which all members and friends of the church were invited. The day was bright and fine; the price of the tickets was sixpence (two and a half pence), the proceeds given to the church funds. Competitive games were held in the garden and a delightful tea served indoors.

June 24th 1939. A garden party tea was held at Lavender Cottage. It may well have been the last occasion this event took place. By the summer of 1940 food rationing had started to take effect on domestic catering and life on the Ridge was altered by the expediencies of war.

1939. In September it was noted in the church accounts by Clare that expenses had been incurred to arrange for blackouts, this had been 'a costly affair'. Later records noted that £3.00 had been spent on materials for this necessity, supplied from London. It was agreed that in future committee meetings would take place immediately after the Sunday morning service. I would imagine that this was to avoid the need to go out in the blackout to attend meetings.

February 1940. The A.G.M. ended with the resolution that 'this congregation shall consider the possibility of supporting one of the many Jews now coming to this country'. The church's records for the next two years are missing.

The letters of thanks for food parcels from Marion, Emilie's cousin in Canada, began in 1942. Emilie wrote almost nothing to Marion about the day-to-day life on the Ridge during the war, certainly with the censor in mind. However, it is possible to illustrate this period of Emilie's life with the childhood recollections of Richard Pitcairn-Knowles, who lived at the Riposo Nature Cure Hydro, just across the road from Lavender Cottage. Although not quite seven years old in September 1939, Richard was aware of the tension and concern among the adults in the household. He continued with his education at Clyde House Kindergarten in Sedlescombe Road North but evacuation soon reduced pupil numbers so drastically that schools closed and thenceforth much of Richard's education was a solitary affair; two days a week with two retired school teachers, the Misses Lock, at Sedlescombe. At times he had no schooling at all. His mother had decided not to evacuate herself and her son from Hastings, so Richard spent long spells of free time at Riposo, roaming its extensive grounds and, as he grew older, the surrounding lanes and countryside, witnessing many enemy raids. German aircraft, crossing the English Channel from France at wave-top height, west of Dover, flew low over the Romney March and on meeting the Ridge, rose to skim Riposo at chimney pot level, going on to bomb the town below.

In 1940 Richard watched the Battle of Britain from the gardens and fields at Riposo, oddly comforted that his father was fluent in German and would be able to speak to the enemy, if they landed. This fluency in German was put to good use on September 25th 1940, when a Hurricane, pursuing and machine gunning a German ME 110, brought the enemy plane down in Beaney's Lane, a muddy track leading from the Ridge to Westfield. It was a near miss for Riposo and for Lavender

Cottage too. Clouds of black smoke could be seen rising from the crashed plane, which had burst into flames. The crew had baled out but the altitude was too low for parachutes to open fully and they lay badly injured in the field, opposite to Landsview Terrace, with a few local villagers standing round each crewman. Richard walked to the field gate with his parents Gordon and Joyce, who told him he could not 'go and gawp' at the injured airmen. Their instructions were reinforced by the police and a fireman in an asbestos suit. Richard's mind was on collecting souvenirs but the wreck was blazing and the plane's ammunition was exploding with cracks and bangs. With his fluent German, Richard's father was able to speak with the injured Luftwaffe pilot, who tore the cross off his uniform and pressed it into the ground with his heel, cursing Hitler and the futility of war, before he died. There was a sombre mood in the Pitcairn Knowles family for the rest of the day, which Richard was too young to understand, his conclusion being that surely, it was the enemy who had crashed? The dead German airmen were Eberhard Weyergang, aged 24 and Gustav Nelson, aged 27; both are buried in Hastings Cemetery.

As the autumn evenings of 1940 set in and the Blitz began on London, Richard was taken along the Ridge to gaze north, where, after dark, the glow of London in flames, fifty miles away, could be clearly seen. He was out alone on one day, by the top of Grange Road where it joins the Ridge, when several German bombers passed overhead, chased by British fighter planes, machine guns blazing. This time he did not stand in the middle of the road and watch as he normally did but hid under a willow tree, in the garden of Yew Tree Cottage. (There is mention of a Yew Tree Farm in records of Magistrates' Court proceedings in winter 1942, when two men were up before the bench for stealing chickens from Mr Novis, who is listed in Kelly's Street Directory as resident at the cottage. As there is no farm on the map for this location it can be presumed it was a smallholding, attached to the cottage; Mr Novis was a tenant of the Pitcairn-Knowles, who at that time owned Yew Tree Cottage). In June 1942 a full-scale, mock invasion was mounted in Hastings and the Ridge was used as a stronghold and manned by troops. Richard remembers seeing the steam roller and men with pneumatic drills, early in 1942, tearing up the old tram lines buried beneath the Ridge road surface and pulling out the strips of metal, 'like long teeth', for the precious scrap metal they provided. The wrought iron railings at the front of Riposo were also sacrificed for munitions. How Emilie must have longed to write to Marion and Beatrice about these dramatic events.

In May 1944, leading up to the June D-day landings, the lanes and tracks around the Ridge were overflowing with lorries, concealed under camouflage nets. Richard, aged 11, cycled round the waiting convoys, counting the increasing numbers of army vehicles. Sometimes on his 'inspections' he would be given chocolate by the soldiers. Richard's parents thought that all this military presence invited German air raids and Richard and his mother went to Chertsey, to stay with family friends for a short time, returning soon after D-Day. Richard recalls seeing in the skies above the Ridge 30 to 40 Lancaster bombers, almost at tree-top level, limping home on just two or three of their four engines, after raids on France. The flying bomb raids started in June 1944. The doodlebugs were launched at a trajectory to clear the North Downs, which are about 700 feet in height, so that when the craft flew over the Ridge their altitude was about 200 feet and the sound of their engines rattled windows; three different flight paths of the doodlebugs passed around the bounds of Riposo and of course Lavender Cottage. From the garden at Riposo Richard saw a Spitfire dive under a doodlebug and lift its right wing, upsetting its balance so that it crashed about a mile away, with a loud explosion. It fell on a house not far from Clyde House School (now a nursing home). Reading Richard's account of the war I wondered how Emilie, Clare and Edith coped with all this; a crashed German aircraft and dead Germans, practically in their back garden, low-level enemy flight paths above the cottage and hordes of military personnel occupying the formerly privately owned mansions and schools along the Ridge. It was certainly not the life that Emilie expected when she retired to live in the countryside.

In 1943 a meeting of Emilie's church committee wrote a letter to the Prime Minister, the Home Secretary and Hastings and St Leonards Member of Parliament, Mr Hely Hutchinson, in which they made a vigorous appeal for help for the Jews in Europe: 'We urge the British Government, in co-operation with all the other united nations, to offer unstilted aid, practical and financial, in rescuing all who can escape from all areas or those threatened by German domination by:

a) Adopting a policy of the open door in this country, in Palestine and in the colonies.

b) Granting transit visas valued for two years ahead.

c) Making grants of food to countries receiving refugees, such as Switzerland and Turkey'.

Literary Society Programme.

On 22nd February 1944 Emilie Crane gave a talk on 'Trees'.

"The gallery was full, with 30 members present for the occasion of Miss Crane's reading of her paper, 'Trees'. Miss Crane, one of our most popular speakers, mentioned at once that she was not speaking as an expert but had been attracted to the subject not only by the beauty and variety of trees but by the legends and myths attached to them. Miss Crane could not only say something about every variety of tree but we heard some interesting things. The early Britons and Celts worshipped the oak and beneath its massive boughs Druids performed their mystic rites...The willow is an emblem of sadness and Miss Crane recalled many ancient references to it from the Old Testament and Shakespeare. Her paper was concluded by a fine tribute to the 'Men of the Trees' and the Voluntary Association for the Preservation of Trees and Forestation".

1944. A committee statement was worded, "This is the fifth year of conflict and we are still living in wartime. Our little church has gone bravely on; full of hope and expectation that this is the year that war will end". It was suggested that on the declaration of peace, on whatever that day occurred, a special church service of thanksgiving should be held at 6.30 that evening.

Dating from February, 1945 the church committee meeting minutes were in Emilie's familiar handwriting, as she became the secretary to the church committee in that year and Clare was re-elected as the treasurer.

Literary Society Meeting Programme. March 28th 1945. Emilie Crane gave a talk on 'Back to Methuselah', the work by George Bernard Shaw. He was something of a favourite with Emilie, mainly because of his fondness for animals.

Minutes of Church committee meeting. During 1946, a church member had made a first visit to her family in France and Holland since before the war. She was shocked at the hardship and deprivation she found there and gave a talk on the subject to the church Women's' League, who sent a parcel of clothing to Holland.

Minutes of Literary Society meeting. On 14th November,1946, twenty-two members of the Literary Society were present to hear Miss Crane give a paper (talk) but sadly, she was unable to come, due to the mortal illness of a friend. Emilie's name appeared from time to time as a speaker but there are no further details of her talks other than the titles:

November 26th 1946 Literary Society Programme. Emilie gave a talk on Fanny Burney.

Minutes of Literary Society committee meeting. On March 7th 1947 Miss Crane telephoned that she had been advised, owing to the danger of falling trees, to stay indoors and therefore could not give her paper. It was certainly a long and bitter winter and Emilie wrote to Marion about the conditions of the Ridge that had kept her indoors:

'...the roads were impassable with snow and ice for three weeks. The sight was magnificent; like a pantomime fairyland. Telephone wires and tree branches were coated thickly with ice; folks came up from the town just to see it. Sadly, birds died by the thousands and telephone poles crashed down into the hedges. Then the rains came and I expect you have read of the havoc that has caused. I do wonder how the farmers have the heart to carry on but the British are very resilient.'

On 9th October 1947.
Emilie was programmed to give a paper on The Human Face by John Brophy but I suspect this did not happen, as a letter in the same period to Marion and Beatrice says:

"..You will think that I am a disgraceful person to get ill again but I am writing this in bed. I have a bronchial cold with head pains and sickness. I feel I am a nuisance but Clare Emily makes no trouble of it. The doctor was not very cheerful as he was starting an illness, now his

son tells me his father has pneumonia badly. It seems to be a wide spread complaint here; they say that the drought is causing much illness. Things are pretty restless all round; it would not surprise me if another election arrived before its time. Sorry to send such a dull letter, perhaps I will be better soon and not so addle-headed..."

October 21st 1948 Literary Society Programme. Emilie Crane spoke on the subject of The Seashore. A letter written the day before her talk says:

"...Your parcel was most delicious surprise, you have sent us so much already but it was a thrill to have it. I could not resist trying the rice immediately. As I think I mentioned in my last letter, Clare has been laid up for just on 8 weeks so I am cook and housekeeper.

I was much intrigued to learn that a rice pudding could be made without milk, our rations have been cut again, and was delighted when it was cooked in 20 minutes; quite soft and so good. Also I sampled one of the jellies; EL is so attached to jellies but they are so poor here. Your butter is a great boon as our ration of that is cut yet again. We also appreciate the ox tongue and suet; the butcher does not send us any suet, perhaps the cows do not furnish it. The spices will add flavour to a recipe that I have found for egg-less cake.

Please forgive my short letter, the first two fingers of my right hand are so sore with arthritis it is difficult to write much. I am having radio treatment and the doctor says he will soon get rid of the pain. It's a family complaint with us; my brother had it very badly but in his time there was no such treatment..."

We now see the arrival into Emilie's church life a person who was to become world famous:

Literary Society Programme. October 6th 1949. Irish Stories read by Mrs Catherine Cookson. That Emilie may not have been present at the meeting on the 6th could be conjectured from a letter dated 17th October 1949

"My Dear Marion and Beatrice,

I know that you will be sorry to hear that Edith Lake passed away on the 9th inst: As I said in my last letter, she had become very incoherent and her head grew worse. We had to get in a nurse for her at nights and later for all day. The end was very sudden. She was unconscious for 4 days and never spoke again, just going peacefully. It was for the best but we miss her terribly. We have hardly grasped yet how this will affect us materially but I will not say anything of that, as I know little of the family's arrangements but I expect we will have to leave Lavender Cottage. However, that would not be very soon, I think. I want to thank you again for your most kind and generous gift, it was most good of you and at this time it will be especially a great help. I have not answered your letter referring to this but I will let you know more later on as to what is happening. I am just going to start another batch of letters received from friends and relatives of Edith, who all appear to have written to us, instead of to the family. Please forgive a short epistle for the present.
My love and good wishes for the new home and renewed thanks for all your thought and kindness.
With very much love,
Emilie"

It was the death of Edith Lake and her failure to attend to the details of her will, with reference to Lavender Cottage and her friends' future that subjected Emilie Crane to six years of uncertainty and insecurity. Literary Society Programme February 23rd 1950. More Irish Stories by Mrs. Catherine Cookson. Emilie wrote at this period:

"...The time of institutional meetings has arrived once more and I have been grousing over annual reports... (Emilie also refers here to her other secretarial work for St Catherine's House Convalescent Home) ... My other annual meeting is for the church and it is quite jolly. I guess Clare will make cakes for the tea.

Folks are very busy about the coming election and there is a great deal of uncertainty as to how the votes will go. A good many say they will not vote at all but I think that is a mistake. Of course, it is trying to have three sets of people competing, as we have in Hastings, especially if you feel sympathetic with two of them. It seems so absurd not to have proportional representation, doesn't it? Our new neighbour will not vote at all but we shall both go to the poll. We listen to the speakers on the wireless very conscientiously; they all promise so much and will probably do so little. Well, I mustn't talk politics, especially when CE is doing accounts. It is so distracting, especially when she is a pound out! I expect the pound will come to her in the night, it usually does; she is the most careful housekeeper. Oh dear! I wish I could write like Beatrice. I was reading one of her articles the other day and envied her the easy flow of the language it contained. When is she going to write a book? We have read one or two American books lately, at least CE has, and she says that they are much better than English novels nowadays. I am not reading any at present, being occupied with meetings and trying to write a paper for our Literary Society.

We both send very much love to you both and hope you are not being frozen. It is hard for us to keep warm at present. The birds eat nearly a loaf a day, poor things."

On 6th October 1950, Mrs Catherine Cookson gave another talk to the Literary Society, no title was stated in the minutes and there is no hint in Emilie's letters whether she attended or not. It may have been that Mrs Cookson's subjects were a bit light-weight for Emilie and Clare, neither of whom seemed to care much for modern literature and there seemed plenty to do on the domestic scene.

Emilie wrote on 13th October 1950:

Dear Marion and Beatrice,

Your letter has just arrived; everything you sent us is so good and acceptable that it is difficult to differentiate but I will do my best, since you have kindly asked. I will put the items, (pretty large "items"), in order of preference.

The butter, tinned bacon, dried milk, sultanas and raisins are invaluable. We only get one egg and two rashers a week each, of inferior quality, and butcher's meat lasts only three days out of seven. Christmas puddings are scarce but we can usually manage to get one.

The fat you send is always totally different from the synthetic lard we get which has to be grated. The pastry and cake powders we can buy here and we are well off for spices.

We did mange to get 1/2 pound of sultanas and raisins and generally we can get dates. Today, we had a pie made from one of your tins of hot-pot, it was real good. Even our cat James approved. It is joyful to think of a turkey, we are already issuing invitations on the strength of it. I think that drawn, (gutted) would be best.

The sugar is most welcome as it has been "cut" again but we are quite well off for it at present as a friend also gave us some she had from Barbados; as soon as the parsnips come in I shall make some wine. There are so many things in the parcel that are useful but I think we have given you a long enough list.

This is a scrappy letter but we though it advisable to write at once in view of what you said so I won't stop to comment on your holiday at present

Yours affectionately,

Emilie"

Catherine Cookson spoke again to the Literary Society on 11th January 1951 on the subject of 'This Writing Business' A report of this talk said: "Mrs Cookson told the meeting that she received seven pence h'penny (4p) per copy of each of her books that sell at 8/6d (43p). She is much touched by the sordid in peoples' lives and gets her material from life in the raw. She is a successful writer of short stories and has just published her first novel, Kate Hannigan, which she said she re-wrote three times and that this novel completely drained her of ideas and emotions. Mrs Cookson said that she believes that correspondence courses are not of much help to would-be writers and that it is better to get help from books and public libraries. She added that all those who attended the meeting must realise the nervous energy spent in this writing business". Apart from a passing reference to the fact that Catherine Cookson lived for a number of years in a house not far from the Ridge, I did not expect to be making further comment on her and was therefore surprised to find her mentioned in the reports of the church literary society speakers. Of course, at that time, Catherine Cookson was little known and the society may not have felt any great sense of privilege in having this newly-published writer speak at their meetings. Catherine's invitation to address the ladies of the UFCC probably came about as a result of the friendship she and her husband Tom shared with the Rev Hilton, the church's minister and his wife, Muriel. Catherine Cookson had been resident in Hastings for some years previous to her appearance before the Women's Literary Society; she arrived in Hastings in 1929, coincidentally the same year as Emilie Crane. Catherine held the job of manageress in the laundry at St Helen's Hospital for three years and her writing career began in middle age, under the encouragement of her schoolmaster husband. In her personal story, Our Kate, she wrote of going on the bus from Parker Road in Hastings to catch the train to see her publisher in London, to discuss her first novel, Kate Hannigan, published in 1950. Her excitement at this prospect made her feel inclined to tell the weary-looking woman sitting beside her on the bus that she was just about to have a book published but felt that that the response might have been, "So what!" This mirrored my own experience over 50 years later, as I travelled home on the number 20 bus, after a visit to my printer at Hollington, with a draft copy of my first book in my handbag. Now-a-days the passenger response, had I mentioned my feelings of excitement about my book would probably be, "Whatever!" (Or something less printable). Catherine Cookson's Kate Hannigan was briefly reviewed in the Hastings and St Leonards Observer in 1950, with a tone of disapproval at the book's frank approach to sex outside marriage and illegitimacy. It's easy to understand, therefore, why it could not be revealed, in those more censorious times, that the story was based on Catherine's own life as an illegitimate child.

Catherine Cookson's talk on This Writing Business may not have been attended by Emilie, as in a letter dated January 17th 1951 she wrote:

"...It seems a very long time since I wrote; I have been trying to send you a letter since Christmas. One cause for delay was that I couldn't get down to town on account of the weather and the local shop is devoid of both air letters and stamps for long intervals. It sounds silly but it is a bit awkward up here, especially when we have snow, as they

never sweep it away. Our neighbours, Miss Feather, the old lady, her invalid and the parrot's mother (Mrs Todd) have all shared in the parcels you sent; I fear that they don't get much in the way of presents. I must tell you how useful the handkerchiefs you sent have been to me. I had a fearful cold after my friend's funeral and as our charlady has been laid up for a month with bronchitis she could not do any washing, it would have been so inconvenient without hankies. The government has cut the meat ration again down to one shilling (5 pence) per person per week. We did not mind that too much as we had your parcels but we do feel a bit annoyed at coal being reduced to one hundredweight per household per week; we burn almost 5 hundredweight in that time. However, we can get logs; I fear that many poor people do not have these. As Clare says; "We are very fortunate." I took a car down to see my old friend in hospital last Sunday; I have to have cars occasionally because of my bad eyesight. I found him rather sad as the doctors are going to amputate his leg. He is a good fellow and one feels very sorry for him. Clare sends her love, as do I, and very best wishes for the New Year..."

Church A.G.M. 1952. 23rd February 1952. The Hon: Sec: Miss E. Crane read her report, which covered all of the activities of the church during the past year and gave notice of several deaths among members and also the illnesses of other members (a probable reference to Clare Marriott, who was suffering from throat cancer), making the numbers at the Sunday services often very small. Miss Crane asked that all should do their utmost to introduce new members. The minutes continued: "It was with the deepest regret that we were compelled to accept the resignation of Miss Crane, who has held office as secretary since 1945 but now has to relinquish it, due to ill-health and other worries. Miss Crane is very revered and loved by all. A small token of our regard was given in the form of a flowering plant".

In one of Emilie Crane's letters dated 24th February 1952 we have her view of the meeting:

..."Yesterday, I had an afternoon off, when a neighbour came to sit with Clare for two hours. It was the Annual General Meeting of our church and I had to go to read my year's report and, sadly, give up my secretary-ship. The church meeting was very nice; they said such kind

things and presented me with a gorgeous pot of flowers and delightful remarks. I stayed to tea after the meeting and when I went to my car they followed me, singing, "For She's a Jolly Good Fellow". They are such nice people. We are giving a swell tea in April for the Women's Club and Literary Society, which I hope to go to if Clare is well enough. It is nice little church and they are all so kind" ...

As her later letters tell, Emilie was overwhelmed with grief at Clare Marriott's death on March 27th 1952 and it is doubtful that she attended the "swell tea".

In mid-September 2004 I had a package and letter from Wendy which was something of a breakthrough in the attempts to trace Emilie Crane's family.

Dear Victoria,

I hope you are as excited about the enclosed as I am. I ordered a copy of Emilie's will at the end of July and it came today. It gives me some family names to work on as well as tying up a few loose ends. It is lovely to see signatures of people whose names we know from Letters from Lavender Cottage. Wouldn't it be wonderful to find some of the descendents of those nieces and the nephew? I think I'll put out some feelers on rootsweb.com and see what happens.

Love from Wendy

Emilie had made a reference to the making of a will in a letter dated June 5th 1952

"I made my will last week and have tried to act fairly towards Clare's relatives, though I must say that they do not wish me to consider them in any way. They are not rich but keep saying they have enough and the two girls are very pleased with the £500 they each get. The nephew and the niece are better off but I thought it only fair to remember them too. The lawyer laughs at me, like Nurse, he thinks I have a money spending capacity and there won't be much left when I have finished".

By 1954 her letters were becoming less frequent and rambling and they did not mention seeing her solicitor. The will Wendy sent to me, dated from 1954, stated that Emilie's much mentioned nephew, Robert Kenneth Crane of 'Grafton' Camden Park Road, Chislehurst, Kent was appointed as her executor and to him she bequeathed £200; the other executor was the solicitor, Charles Harding.

Emilie requested that all her articles of personal use, ornament and enjoyment should be distributed by Robert K Crane according to any instructions she left. She made a number of bequests to various nieces and nephews. True to her word, she bequeathed specific sums to a nephew of Clare Marriot, and divided the remainder of her estate between Clare's two nieces.

Emilie bequeathed £50 to the Reverend Denbigh Hilton, the minister at the Hastings Unitarian Free Christian Church, Hastings. Emilie also left to the church the sum of twenty-five pounds, thus giving me the clue to the denomination of the 'nice little church' to which she referred in her letters and proving the error in my first supposition that St Peter's, The Ridge, the 'tin tabernacle' on the Ridge was Emilie's place of worship. She also left £25 to the United Free Christian Church at Brixton and £25 to Catherine House, the convalescent home for elderly gentlewomen, on whose committee she had served faithfully for so many years. Emilie's love of animals was reflected in her bequest of £50 to the People's Dispensary for Sick Animals, the sum to be divided equally between the London and Hastings Branches.

The will is witnessed by Mrs E. G Cole of 10, Charles Road, St Leonard's on Sea and R S Arfield, of 408a, The Ridge, which was the extension built onto Lavender Cottage in 1951. Mrs Cole was the lady from Emilie's Church, who looked after her. A codicil to the will dated 29th June 1954 adds a further beneficiary, to receive the sum of £50, a David Heulin of 7, Avondale Road, St Leonards on Sea. The codicil is witnessed in youthful handwriting by a Miss Rosemary A Cruttenden, 156, Victoria Avenue, Hastings, shorthand typist. By a series of convoluted enquires in which luck and coincidence played a considerable part, I tracked down Rosemary, now in her seventies; sadly, she could not recall Emilie. It had been Rosemary's duty, while in the employ of Solicitors Harding and Horrox of 7, Trinity Street Hastings, to witness so many wills and none were memorable.

A further codicil to Emilie's will was added on 22nd November 1954, in which she revoked her former legacy of £50 to the Reverend Denbigh Hilton and in its place left him £20. We can only guess at why the original sum of the bequest to the Reverend was reduced. Maybe he came to hear of it and it was altered at his request. He must have known of Emilie's extreme generosity, which became rather flamboyant in her declining years; perhaps he thought the greater sum unseemly in the circumstances. The second codicil is witnessed by Grace C Mann, Lavender Cottage, 408a, The Ridge, Hastings. Grace Mann's occupation was noted as a companion but it would seem she did not carry out that duty to Emilie. She may well, however, have been the person who brought Emilie's days at Lavender Cottage to a close, by some means never clearly specified, other than in the confused details in Emilie's final few letters, before her death. Her last letter, post marked 27th May 1955 was sent from Bleaton House and is full of gaps and digressions:

Please forgive this scrawl my head still....felt funny.......must write ....you didn't ans... my last I felt you must be vexed somewhat. Was it about Bob....very good if it is business affairs but does not much ....I hadn't seen much of the girls for some time April have got so poorly There are so many now for the.... I don't know ....names But I send things being............now have been sending girls gifts for her for some time. I went out some time back but it is ...so one can't go often especially now one's feet are so bad. Perhaps you think I spent all the money you so kindly sent me on myself but I kept a share each for Clare and the others and I have sent the West ones girls £60 and clothes and things and the boys something but they do well at work . I don't know a number of the others but will send some to Olive because she is ill. I must end this letter because I can't write yet.

The last line is illegible.

Emilie was moved to a nursing home at 18, St Helen's Crescent, a short distance from Bleaton House, where she died on 11th September 1955. She had steadfastly refused the invitations of her family to go and live with them, apparently feeling she was under some obligation to stay in Hastings. There is no way of knowing if her reason was medical, her attachment to the memory of the years spent in the area with her dear friend Clare or the independence that was so much part of her character. Readers of the book Letters from Lavender Cottage felt saddened by Emilie's lonely death, as I did.

The details in Emilie's will led to Wendy Johnson discovering a branch of her family that she never expected to know. Among them was a 14 year old girl called Emily Crane. This youthful Emily, spelled with a 'y', is resident in America; we have met only via email. I asked her if she would like to tell me something about herself to bring the story of Emilie Crane's family into the 21st century.

Emily Crane replied:

Dear Victoria,

First off, I'd like to say that I'm very excited to be involved with the sequel. Thank you for including me. I haven't read Letters from Lavender Cottage yet, but when I've finished a reading assignment for school I'll start it. It shouldn't be too long! I got your email that has the interview, and thought I'd give it a little bit more thought before sending it off. My dad sent you a picture of me. Again, thank you for including me and I'm looking forward to working with you.

Best wishes,

Emily Crane

From the exchange of emails that constituted the interview I learned that Emily Crane was born in Gravesend England on the 25th April 1991; she went to live in the USA a year later and was subsequently educated under the public system in Georgia. At school she enjoys science and history, particularly WWII history and also likes drawing and music. She has not yet decided on a career but is interested in Criminal Justice. Emily likes to spend her free time doing normal 'girl things' with her friends, of whom she says: 'We always have great times together, I love them'. Emily enjoys swimming and it comes easily to her but she is not on a team as she sees it as a big commitment. During the school holidays she visits her family in England with her brother Robert and they go out into the countryside. Emily likes to read youth-orientated and history-related literature, by English authors. She says of herself that she is an extrovert and, unlike her great-great-great Aunt Emilie Crane, she would like to get married one day.

Emily's parents say of her:

"She is very observant, creative, self-confident, and articulate. She seems quite wise to the ways of the world for one so young and gets

impatient when she sees people who don't do their jobs as well as she thinks they should!"

Wendy Johnson has added this postscript to Emilie's life

"Perhaps some people will think that Emilie Crane's life was unremarkable, and in a sense it was. However, as my family and I read her letters and got to know her through them, her personality and character have become very dear to us. We are grateful to Victoria for pursuing Emilie's life as it has been revealed since the publication of Letters from Lavender Cottage".

PART TWO

EMILIE'S PLAY

In Emilie's Lavender Cottage letter dated July 23rd 1948 she said that she once had a 'scholastic' letter printed in The Times and a play she had written was published in the Boy's Own Paper. Wendy Johnson said that she had spent thousands of dollars in air fares and many hours in research, including those at London's British Library, to track down this play and she finally succeeded in finding it in October 2003. She particularly wished it to appear in this book.

A little history of the Boy's Own Paper may give a guide as to possibly why Emilie Crane chose this magazine as a vehicle for her play. The BOP was founded in 1879, first edited by G. A. Hutchinson and published at the price of one penny per week by the Religious Tract Society. The purpose of the society, which began in 1779, was to disseminate Christian literature of both an Anglican and nonconformist nature. The purpose of the Boy's Own Paper was to provide a wholesome alternative to the bloodthirsty, 'penny dreadfuls' that were so popular at the time. Hutchinson's years of editorship were characterized by a tone of Christian morality and the inclusion of boys of all social backgrounds. But by 1890 poorer readers were sidelined and the content of the paper was aimed at public and grammar school boys. The paper covered a wide variety of subjects; hobbies, sport, care of pets, adventure stories and, on a personal note, how to grow a moustache! Contributors to the paper were nonentities like Emilie or the famous; sportsmen, W G Grace and Jack Hobbs and writers, Jules Verne, Joseph Conrad and R M Ballantyne. The principles promoted by the Boy's Own Paper had a lasting effect on boys of all ages; it is said that the paper was read in the trenches. After WWI the article content moved with the times; wireless building, gun-making and mine-laying. The paper had a keen readership throughout the 1920s and into the 1930s. The BOP was bought by Lutterworth Press in 1939 and thenceforth, no doubt due in part to the effects of war, the paper went into decline and never really recovered. The last edition was published in 1967. It was inevitable that the Boy's Own Paper would appeal to Emilie Crane, it was middle-class, nonconformist and had a close association with the kind of boys to whom her career was dedicated.

The date of the edition of the Boy's Own Paper, in which Emilie's play was published, was February 1921, the month of her 50th birthday. The subtitle, A Breaking-up Piece', indicates it was an entertainment to be performed by the pupils at the end of a school term, a very common event at one time. The heading picture of boys playing football bears no relation to the subject of the play and it was probably used just to catch the young reader's attention. There is no clue as to who drew the figures to illustrate the characters in the play. The performance is set in a city office and it depicts the comical struggles of the boss to find a suitable office boy. Emilie may well have drawn on her Victorian workplace for inspiration for the scene-setting but it is her quirky sense of fun that shines through the plot. The image of the Boy's Own Paper front cover for April 1921 was a rare and remarkable find. I hope it will be forgiven that the edition illustrated herein was published two months after Emilie's play.

The Boy's Own Paper. February 1921 Volume XLIII Part 4

"Boy Wanted" A Breaking-up Piece by E. E. Crane.

CHARACTERS.

MR GUMBLENAG. (A business man).
THE LIVELY BOY.
THE SLOW BOY.
THE DEMON KING.
THE PERFECTLY PERFECT BOY.
MR ABRAHAM NOAH (a client of MR GRUMBLENAG.)
AUNT MARIA (MR GRUMBLENAG'S maiden aunt.)

Scene: A city office. To the left, a table with papers, circulars, envelopes, inkstand, box for stamps and a bell.

Left Centre, MR GRUMBLENAG'S coat and hat hanging on a peg. Right centre, an imitation telephone; chairs, long broom in corner;

duster and stove brush in convenient place.

MR GRUMBLENAG discovered sitting at a table reading a letter. He places it in an envelope, directs it, and looks round, then takes out his watch.

MR. G. Ten o'clock and not a boy turned up yet. How on earth am I going to get anything done without a soul to run an errand or mind the office? (In a grumbling tone) Not that boys are any good when one does get them! Always got the face-ache when there's work to be done; making themselves ill gorging sweet stuff all day long and want to go and bury their grandmothers every time there's a football match on! I don't know what boys are coming to! When I was a boy - (knock heard) Ah, There's someone-perhaps it's a boy after the situation. (another knock.) Come in! (Enter the LIVELY BOY, rather dirty, very untidy but sharp-looking.)

MR G. Well, who are you?

L. B. (with strong Irish accent) Plaze sorr, I'm a bhoy.

MR G. I can see that you aren't a girl. What do you want?

L. B. Plaze sorr, I've come after the place.

MR G. Come after the place, have you? Have your brought your references?

L. B. Plaze sorr, me mother says me rifernces is in me face.

MR G. Well, my lad, perhaps if you'd washed your face a bit more, I might have been able to see them. Anyway, what can you do?

L. B. Me mother says I kin do anything sorr.

MR G. Oh, no doubt your mother thinks you're an angel! Most mothers do.

L. B. No sorr, plaze sorr, -she calls me a little varmint mostly.

MR G. All boys are that but I don't suppose you are any worse than the rest of them. I don't as a rule take a boy with out a character, but as you look pretty bright I am willing to give you a trial.

L.B. Thank ye, sorr.

MR. G. You had better begin right away: there's plenty to do. Suppose you take that duster and give the place a good dust up. It hasn't been done since my last boy went.

(MR. G. goes on with his work while the LIVELY BOY takes duster and begins dusting with the utmost rapidity; he dashes at the chairs and dusts them, falling over in the process; he dusts the telephone, the walls, the floor and MR G.'s overcoat and then starts on MR. G.'s top hat, taking it off the peg and rubbing it vigorously-MR G. looks up)

MR.G. (angrily). What are you doing, you clumsy young idiot? Don't you know how to treat a gentleman's hat? Don't touch it with that dirty rag. Give it a good brush if you want to. That won't hurt it. (goes on reading).

L. B. Yis, sorr. (looks round, sees the stove brush, picks it up and begins brushing the hat with it, pretending to spit on it as he brushes. The hat begins to assume the appearance of the 'fretful porcupine'. MR.G. looks up again).

MR G. (jumping up angrily and snatching the hat away).You silly nincompoop! What are you doing? You've ruined the hat! Goodness gracious, isn't it possible to get hold of a boy with a grain of sense in him? My only decent hat! (smoothing it as he speaks) And Aunt Maria will be here soon and I'll have to take her out to lunch! Oh, you idiot! (Telephone rings) There, go and answer the telephone.

L.B. Yis, sorr. (goes to the telephone, looks at it, scratches his head, shakes it and looks at MR G.; the telephone bell ringing all the while).

MR G. What, don't you know how to answer the telephone yet? Take the receiver off the hook and put it to your ear. The receiver donkey, that thing there!(Comes to the telephone and lifts the receiver.) Hold it to your ear like that and put your mouth to the speaking- tube. (gives the boy the receiver). Now, answer the person politely.

L.B. Yis sorr. (speaking through the tube) Halloo yerself! (listens, and turns round) Plaze sorr, it's a femile lidy and she says, "Are ye there dear?"

MR G. (who has take up his papers again) Well, well, answer her.

L.B.(shouts into the tube). Yis, me old darlin', meself's here!

MR G. (jumping up). What's that? What are you saying? Here, come away from there. (pushes boy aside and takes the receiver). No, no, my dear-nothing of the sort-I assure you - it's that new boy of mine-now do listen to me! You're quite wrong my dear-it's all a mistake-no one ever dreamed of such a thing-oh well- if you won't listen-(hangs up receiver with a despairing look and turns to the boy) Now you've done it, you precious piece of brightness! That's my wife and she's in a pretty tantrum. Says I've put someone up to insult her and has gone into hysterics. Won't there be row when I get home? As if I hadn't enough to worry me without this. Well, you've done enough mischief for one day. The sooner you get out of this the better it will be for you. Look sharp and get out! Go home and tell your mother to try and knock a little sense into you with a good-sized broom handle! D' ye hear?

L.B. Yis, sorr. (Exit).

MR. G. (pacing the room) There goes another of them! They're all alike, not a pin to choose between them for ignorance and stupidity. Now what am I to do? Here's the morning nearly gone and not a stroke of work done. All these circulars to get off today and not a letter answered! (clutches his hair) And Noah will be along in a minute or two after the money I owe him and how am I to put him in a good temper with my nerves like fiddle-strings? It's enough to drive a man mad! (throws himself into his chair, and leans his head on his hand. A heavy dragging sound is heard outside and then the noise of someone falling against the door. Enter the SLOW BOY, dragging his feet along the floor. He is a lumpish-looking youth, with a vacant look in his eyes and his mouth open in a wide grin. He comes up to the table).

MR.G. (looking up.) Well, what do you want?

S. B. (in a hoarse voice). A've come arter the job.

MR G. Well, why don't you take your hat off when you are speaking to a gentleman?

(The S.B. removes his hat slowly with both hands and puts it down on MR G's. paper's.)

MR G. Not there stupid! Hang it up.

(The S.B. goes to the wall and tries to hang his hat on a peg; it falls off. After several attempts, during which he looks round at the audience and grins, he manages to persuade the hat to stay on the peg).

S.B.(to the world in general.)That's my best 'at, that is, and mother told me to be very careful with that there 'at. (He comes back to the table, brings a large apple out of his pocket and takes a huge bite out of it).

MR G. What are you doing? Haven't you had any breakfast this morning?

S.B. Yus, but me mother says a'm a growin' lad and wants feedin' up.

MR. G. Oh, well, you can't be fed up here, unless it's with work! Put that away at once.

(S.B. stuffs the apple in his pocket reluctantly, wipes his mouth with the back of his hand and grins at MR.G.)

MR. G.(aside). What a boy, he's a perfect fool! (Aloud) So you've come after the situation; do you know anything about the duties of an office boy?

S. B. Naw!

MR. G. Say, "No, sir."

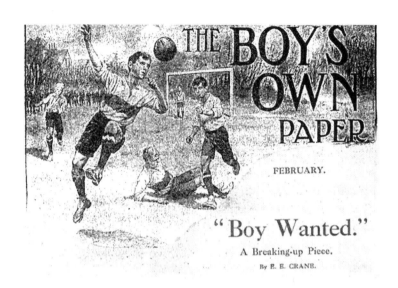

THE **BOY'S OWN PAPER**

FEBRUARY.

"Boy Wanted."

A Breaking-up Piece.

By E. E. CRANE.

Aunt Maria.

The Lively Boy.

Mr. Grumblenag.

The Perfectly Perfect Boy.

S. B. "Naw, sir."

MR. G. Well, that's honest at any rate. Have you brought your references?
(The S. B. stares vacantly at MR. G., scratches his head, then pulls out the contents of his pockets and lays them on the table; the gnawed apple, some string, a piece of bread and butter, pocket knife, etc, etc.)

S. B. Them's all I brought with me.

MR.G. Great Scott! Are you an idiot boy? Don't you know what references are? (The S. B. shakes his head slowly.)

S. B. Are they them things as goes to football matches?

MR G. (impatiently) Football matches! There, it's no use talking to you. I can quite see you won't be an ounce of good but if you like to stay for the day and make yourself useful we'll see how you get on. I've got to have a boy of some sort, and you may turn out better than you look. Here (holding out a letter he has written) I want this to go to the post at once. You'll find a stamp in that box. (The S. B. takes the letter, looks at it, goes to the box, picks out a stamp and brings it and the letter back to MR. G.)

MR. G. (irritably) I don't want it, stupid. Stick on yourself!

(The S. B. looks at MR. G., looks at the letter, looks at the stamp, looks at MR G. again and ends by sticking the stamp on his own cheek.)

MR. G. (jumping up). What are you doing? Give me the letter, booby. (snatches letter). Oh, you'll drive me mad. Here, sit down and see if you can't do something properly. Fold these circulars and put them in these envelopes; they must be got off today. I suppose you can do a simple thing like that without making a fool of yourself?

(MR. G. resumes his work. The S. B. picks up half-a-dozen circulars at once, crushes them together and tries to squeeze them into an envelope. The envelope splits; he throws it on the floor and takes another, with the same result. After doing this several times he manages to get the circulars in, licks the flap and thumps it on the table with a mighty bang. MR. G. looks up.)

Mr. G. Whatever are you up to? (picks up the envelope and tears it open) Why, you everlasting noodle, you've sent six circulars to one man? Don't you know better than that? And look at the mess you've made of them! Do you call that folding? Haven't you got any common-sense at all? (looks down and sees the floor strewn with torn envelopes) Oh, that's the limit! Get out of my office you great hulking lout; you're ten thousand times worse than the other one! Take your hat and clear out! D'ye hear me? Don't stand gaping at me! Get out!
(The S. B. goes slowly to the peg, takes his hat, smooths it and puts it on his head then edges towards the door, grinning all the time.) Get a move on and don't grin at me or I'll give you something to make you grin in a different fashion! (The S.B. goes out, still grinning.)

MR. G. (throwing himself in a chair and wiping his forehead). Did anyone ever come across such a hopeless noodle? Is it possible that in the whole wide world there isn't a single boy with a particle of common-sense in him? Talk of the march of progress! Why on earth doesn't someone invent an automatic boy who will do as he is told and only what he is told; who won't stuff himself all day long with toffee and green apples; won't bury his grandmother twice a week in the football season, and above all who can't say more than, "Yes, sir" and " No, sir"! Oh, I'm sick of the whole race of boys. I feel as tired as a dog after what I have gone through this morning. (Yawns and stretches himself) Suppose I must set to and do the work myself-confound these boys! (Getting sleepier.) Aunt Maria and Noah will be in soon. (his head nods and he drops off into a doze, muttering) Confound all boys-rascally lot-all idiots!

THE DREAM.

(The lights go down. A bang is heard off. Enter the DEMON KING with the PERFECTLY PERFECT BOY, who walks rigidly and automatically. Mr. G. looks up but it must be understood that he is supposed to be asleep and dreaming.)

D. K. (presenting the boy to Mr. G.)

This is the Perfectly Perfect Boy:

He can't do anything to annoy;

He can't eat apples, or sweets or cake,

Because his inside's of clockwork make

He's always neat and he's always clean;

He's seldom heard though he may be seen;

He can't be cheeky, because, you know

He can't say more than "yes" or "no";

If you wind him up in the morning-so (winding Boy.)

The whole day long he'll keep on the go;

If you treat him with care, you'll find him a joy.

(aside) I wonder!

Because he's a perfectly perfect boy!

(Exit the D. K. accompanied by another bang).

Mr. G. (staring at the P.P. Boy) Well. I didn't quite catch all the gentleman said but I understand you are a perfectly perfect boy?

P.P.B. (in a squeaky voice) Yes, sir.

Mr G. And are you sure you know your work?

P. P. B. No, sir.

Mr. G. Eh! What do you mean?

P.P.B. Yes.sir.

Mr. G. That's better. Well you can't be worse than the other specimens I've had here and there's one thing about you-you do look clean. Almost too clean for a boy. How many times a day do you wash your face-a dozen times?

P.P.B. No, sir.

Mr. G. Half-a dozen?

P.P.B. Yes, sir.

Mr. G. Good gracious, what a boy! Washes his face six times a day! I begin to think I've found a treasure at last. Now my lad let's see what you can do. For a start, suppose you take a broom and clear up all this litter on the floor.

(Mr. G. turns to his papers and the P.P. B. walks stiffly to the broom, holds it rigidly and begins sweeping the floor. Presently the broom collides with Mr. G's chair and after the fashion of clockwork toys when they meet an obstacle, the P.P.B. keeps jerking it against the chair. Mr. G. looks round.)

Mr. G. Oh you want me to move, do you?
(moves himself and the chair to the side of the table. P.P.B. follows him up with broom; business repeated until Mr G. gets fidgety.)
Mr. G. There, that will do! (aside) Goes a bit to extremes this boy but at any rate he seems thorough.

(P.P.B. replaces broom)

Mr. G. (aloud) You might run round to the post office with this letter and bring back some more stamps while you are about it-I shall want them. No, stop, on second thoughts I'll go myself- a breath of air will do me good. You can be putting these circulars in while I'm out. (puts on his hat and coat) Before I go, just listen, and be sure not to forget what I am going to say.

P.P.B. No sir.

Mr. G. I'm expecting a gentleman to call this morning, a Mr. Abraham Noah. You'll know him by his clothes; he always wears a rather gaudy tie and a big tie-pin. Also he has a decided nose. I don't particularly want to see him and you may tell him you don't know when I'll be back -say it's uncertain and then perhaps he won't wait. If you can manage to get him out of the office before I return, I shall be uncommonly glad.

P.P.B. Yes, sir.

Mr. G. I don't mind telling you, as you seem a sensible sort of boy, that I owe him some money, and it isn't quite convenient to pay him just now.

P.P.B. No Sir.
Mr. G. (aside) A very intelligent boy this! (aloud) Now if a lady should call-I'm expecting one- a rather elderly lady dressed in a peculiar style, you must be very careful what you say to her.
P. P. B. Yes, sir.

Mr. G. You see, that lady's my aunt and I specially want to see her. So mind you make her take a chair and keep her till I come back - whatever you do, don't let her go.

P.P. B. No, Sir.

Mr. G. I see you quite understand (aside). Really, a most sensible boy! (aloud) Well, now I'm off.

(Takes up his stick and exits. The P.P.B. sits at the table and begins folding the circulars, in a jerky fashion. Enter Mr. Abraham, a flashily dressed gentleman, with a large nose).

Mr. N. Well, my young buck, guv' nor in?

P.P.B. Yes, sir.

Mr. N. Well, tell him Mr. Noah's here and wishes to speak to him.

P.P.B. No, sir.

Mr. N. No, not "No" Noah; N-O-A-H-Noah, do you understand?

P.P.B. Yes, sir.

Mr. N. Well, be off and find him. I can't hang about all day waiting for him. Get a move on you! (boy walks off) What a rum walk that chap has! Looks as if he's worked by a propeller!

(Mr. N. wanders round the room, looks at papers on the table, picks up a circular and reads it; gets impatient, looks at his watch and goes to door.)

Mr. N. Come on, young fellow; are you going to be all day?

(the P.P.B. returns.)

Mr. N. Well, is he coming?

P.P.B. No, sir.

Mr. N. What d'ye mean? Did you give him my message?

P.P.B. Yes, sir.

Mr. N. And what did he say?

P.P. B. No, sir.

Mr. N. "No, sir," indeed! What sort of an answer is that? Like his impudence! I'll " no, sir " him! Does he think I'm going to advance him my hard-earned money and only charge him ninety-nine per cent interest to be put off with an answer like that! What does he take me for? Does he think I'm a fool?

P.P.B. Yes, sir,

Mr. N. I'll "yes sir" you, you impertinent young sauce-box. Take that! (boxes P.P.B's. ear. Boy's arm jerks out automatically and knocks Mr. N. down.)

Mr. N. (getting up and furious) You young scoundrel, how dare you? (rushes at boy who again knocks him down. After more business of this sort, Mr. N. is driven towards the door, shaking his fist and shouting.) I'll have the law on you for this and on your master too. He's put you up to this. But I'll teach the pair of you a lesson. I'll have my money out of him in double quick time. Tell him he needn't expect any mercy from me. I'll show him. (As he backs out, shaking his fist at the Boy he nearly knocks over an elderly lady, dressed in mid-Victorian style, who is just entering.) My Dear Madam, a thousand pardons! I did not see you! I trust I have not hurt you?

Aunt Maria. (a little flustered but dropping a genteel curtsey.) No sir, thank you, not at all.

Mr. N. (raising his hat). It's very good of you to say so, Madam; I can assure you it was quite unintentional, my knocking into you like that.

A. M. Please don't mention it sir. (another curtsey).

Mr N. Good morning, madam.

A.M. Good morning, sir.

(Mr. N. goes off with final shake of his fist at the boy).

A.M. (taking a large fan from a reticule, which she carries, and fanning herself) Boy, is my nephew, Mr. Grumblenag in?

P.P.B. No, sir.

A.M. (indignantly) What do you mean by calling me sir, you jackanapes? "Sir" indeed! Don't you know how to talk to a lady? Do I look like a man?

P.P.B. Yes, sir.

A.M. How dare you? A man indeed! And I, a respectable maiden lady that has hardly looked at a man in her life! To be likened to a nasty, dirty, smoky man! Men! Why, I wouldn't touch the best of them with a red hot poker! Thank goodness I never had anything to do with men.(coyly) Not but what they were much attracted to me in my younger days and even now I fancy I have my share of good looks! (sharply) What are you grinning at boy? Don't you believe me?

P.P.B. No, sir.

A.M. Oh, this boy will drive me mad! What does my nephew mean by having such a boy about the place? Does he keep you here to insult visitors?

P.P.B. Yes, sir.

A.M. This is perfectly outrageous! I won't stay here a minute longer. You tell my nephew when he comes in, young man, that I shall expect a full explanation of your conduct, and an ample apology from him before I set foot in his office again. I was never so treated in my life. (She is going off when the P.P.B. gets in front of her and holds out his arms stiffly to prevent her exit).

A. M. What are you doing? Let me pass at once! Oh, the boy's stark, staring mad!

(P.P.B. and A. M. dodge about, until finally the Boy drives the old lady into a chair, where he holds her down; she shrieks and utters protests but finally collapses into a state of terrified quietness. Enter Mr. G in a state of agitation; he does not see the others at first.)

Mr. G. I can't think what has happened to upset Noah. Wonder why he wouldn't stop and speak to me just now-just shook his fist in my face and went off muttering about having the law on me! Evidently he'd just come from here-I hope that boy of mine didn't say anything to upset him-it would be frightfully awkward if he insists on having his money just now-

(A.M gives a terrified gasp Mr. G. looks round.)

Mr. G. Aunt Maria! What are you doing to the lady you young idiot? Let her go at once. (pulls Boy away.)

A.M. (getting up in a tremendous rage). Don't talk to me! Don't talk to me! I have never been so insulted in my life. You did this on purpose Charles Grumblenag; you set that boy on to insult me, I know you did! This is one of your silly jokes, is it? You won't find it much of a joke though! I'll be even with you! I'll make you suffer for it! I'll cut you off with a shilling, yes I will! I'll leave all my money to the Society for the Propagation of Pug Dogs! Not a penny do you get and don't you think it!

(pushes Mr. G. aside and goes off muttering) Not a single penny - never was so insulted!

Mr. G. (clasping his head despairingly) Good Heavens! What has happened to me? What a horrible state of things! Noah frantic with rage for some reason or other and Aunt Maria gone to cut me off with a shilling! I must be having a bad dream. (to P.P.B.) And you're the cause of it, you bag of unutterable idiocy! I suppose it was you who upset Noah when he called? Didn't you behave civilly to him?

P.P.B. No, sir.

Mr. G. I thought as much! Well, it will please you to know that you've ruined me. I'm done for if he calls his money in. I shan't be able to borrow any from Aunt Maria, that's certain! And she won't leave me a penny in her will, either! Here's a pretty state of things! This is what comes of taking on a Perfectly Perfect Boy! Why wasn't I satisfied with the ordinary sort of boy, who just did the ordinary sort of damage- spoilt my things and got on my nerves and tried my temper! He wouldn't have let me in for this at any rate. I've half a mind to break your head for you! (makes a move towards the Boy, who shoots out his arm and knocks Mr. G. into his chair. Mr. G. stares at him helplessly. The stage grows dark. Bang heard off. Enter the DEMON KING).

D. K.

My automatic boy, I find,

Has failed to meet approval;

And so it just remains to me

To hasten his removal.

But ere we go, a parting word

To you who seek perfection:

It won't be found in any boy

Of whom you make selection.

 "Boys will be boys" - remember that,

Have patience with their blunders;

With all their faults, they're better than

Your automatic wonders.

And for the rest, take comfort, for

Things aren't just what they seem:

Awake and find what's past to be

No other than a dream!

(Exeunt D. K. and P. P. B. Lights)

Mr. G. (waking and looking about him in a dazed fashion.)

A dream! Only a dream! Then it hasn't all happened. There never was a Perfectly Perfect Boy! Noah didn't shake his fist in my face and say he'd have the law on me! And Aunt Maria hasn't been and she hasn't cut me off with a shilling and left all her money to the Society for the

Propagation of Pug Dogs. Thank goodness! Only a dream! But what a nightmare! Phew! No more Perfectly Perfect Boys for me! He's taught me a lesson, anyhow and one I shan't forget in a hurry. Automatic obedience by itself is about as useful as an addled egg and can do a lot more harm. In future I'll stick to the ordinary common or garden boy and make the best of him and his blunders. Now, let's get to work. (takes up his papers.)

Curtain.

PART THREE

EMILIE'S LONG ROAD

The Ridge, the scene of Emilie Crane's final home, is the long and ancient road that stretches from Ore Village to the market town of Battle, wherein lies the site of the Battle of Hastings. Prehistoric man must have trod this elevated track, which at one point is 500 feet above sea level, thus giving travellers safety from the dangers of the swamps and thick forests below. Archaeological excavations along the Ridge have unearthed flint implements, traces of ancient British tribes, and the remains of Roman habitation. In May 1989 a hoard of 92 Roman bronze coins was found on a site near the Ridge, at a location described with deliberate vagueness as 'Ore', in order to discourage amateurs with metal detectors. Shortly thereafter a further 52 silver Roman coins and seven dinarii were found. The British Museum's Roger Bland said that the hoard would have been worth about £50 in Roman times. Land for building on the Ridge did not become available until the early part of the 19th century, when parts of it were sold by Sir Godfrey Webster of Battle Abbey to Edward Milward of Hastings. The new landlord sold on plots for development, on the condition that houses built there must stand in no less than one acre of ground, to keep the area exclusive. Until Milward came into ownership the Ridge was agricultural land, home for generations to only a church, widely-separated farm houses, labourers' hovels and windmills. The homes of farm labourers were not generally built of enduring materials. A description of a cottage that once stood on Broomgrove in the early 1900s gives some idea of the materials used. 'The walls of the cottage were made of cow manure and straw, which was plastered over and then whitewashed. In the summer the house used to swarm with flies and the kitchen ceiling would be black with them'. A significant property constructed on the newly acquired land at the eastward end of the Ridge was Coghurst Hall, built for Brisco Musgrave in 1836, who had come into possession of the estate by marriage. The hall was set in woodland at least two miles from the main road but the Hall's Tudor-style, lodge gatehouse stood on the Ridge highway.

The Ridge in the 1930s was very rural and regarded almost as an outpost of Hastings; it was not without reason that contemporary, foot-patrol police officers referred to the area as the Klondike. Although Emilie heads a letter dated 1934, 'Lavender Cottage, The Ridge', the street maps of the time referred to it as Old London Road. In 1970 the topographer Lawrence P Burgess wrote an article, The Ridge, An Ancient Highway, for the magazine Sussex Life, creating a picture of a road which, unknown to him at the time, was on the brink of major changes that have totally altered its character, from rural peace to constantly busy thoroughfare.

THE HARROW BRIDGE AND BALDSLOW VILLAGE

For the purposes of this reminiscence we begin the journey along the Ridge at Baldslow Village and the Harrow Bridge, which was built in about 1840, in order to cut three miles from the eight hour coach ride to London. Three years after the end of WWII the bridge was the focus of a drama that brought a brief period of excitement to the small village. One morning in 1948, Hastings Police received an urgent telephone call from the Royal Engineers, stationed in a unit in North Sussex. An R. E. officer explained that for some time he had been engaged in checking that all the anti-invasion demolition explosives had been cleared away. He had discovered that the high explosive charges buried under the foundations of the Harrow Bridge had never been cleared. A section of Sedlescombe Road North and the Ridge highway were immediately closed and the occupiers of properties near the bridge were kept at a safe distance, while the explosives were safely removed.

In less than three decades the Harrow Bridge, or Harrow Arch as it is known locally, was under demolition. Its mere 15 feet-wide opening across the A21 from London was causing traffic bottle-necks and in January 1971 the work to remove the bridge began. There was some hostility to the destruction of the bridge from locals, who felt that a simple widening of the arch would solve the problem; they were amused to observe it proved to be no easy matter to remove the sturdy old construction, even with modern demolition devices. The work was impeded by heavy winter rains, which loosened the soil on the steep banks at either side of the bridge; the waste soil was removed to Hole

The Harrow Arch, the summer before its demolition

Baldslow butcher's shop c.1986

Baldslow Village, the Harrow Pub and windmill c.1915

View westwards, The Harrow. c.1910

Farm at Westfield. The new bridge, weighing 700 tons was completed at the cost of £104,000; it had a span of 150 feet, with a 24 foot wide carriage way and two six-foot wide pavements. Present at the bridge official opening on 20th October 1971 were Alderman T. Mears, Chairman of the Hastings Council Works Committee, Mayor H Farley Paine, Hastings Town Councillors and Corporation Officers. In the mid-1960s, Red Lane at Baldslow, which previously was little more than a bridle path, was re-made into the busy Harrow Lane we know today and developed with housing and business units. The mud created by the major works caused the locals such misery it became the topic of letters and articles in the local newspaper.

The arrival of the new road and bridge inevitably brought change to the Baldslow community. Isolated but not particularly wealthy, the village had enjoyed an atmosphere of peace and unity for generations; for most of its daily needs it was self-sufficient. Baldslow resident, Mrs Esther Carpenter, who grew up in the village in the 1940s, compiled a list of its shops for that period: "The post office was run by Cliff and Dorothy Luck, Easton's corner shop by Charles Easton and his wife. A general store with a telephone exchange was run by Jack and Bessie Henson and Mr Hicks and his sons had a bakery, from where they delivered bread to Hollington and as far as Westfield, by horse and cart. The house 811, the Ridge was built by Jack Henson's brother who was known as 'Shish'. At this property he constructed sheds and garden furniture and he rented a plot on the corner of Maplehurst Road, belonging to the Harrow Inn, to display his goods. At Bridge House Mrs Scotcher sold sweets from her front room and neighbour Mr Chapman ran a plant nursery. The Misses Cheeseman occupied 814A the Ridge and operated a laundry from an outbuilding that had been a barrel store for the Harrow Inn. At number 806 Mrs Ebden organised a reading room and the same building housed a mortuary, a curious combination of uses! The butcher's shop, built by Mr Payton, was run by his unmarried daughter". In his article Burgess describes the butcher's shop as having, 'a rustic, rose-embowered veranda, a truly musical-comedy shop.' The altitude of this point on the Ridge made it the ideal spot for a windmill; Baldslow Mill was built by Upfields of Catsfield in 1857; following the loss of the mill's sails in 1900 it continued to grind by steam power until 1920. In the early 1930s it was converted into a private house and it now adds to the charm of this particular spot, as does the Memory House, (once known as Mill House), which in the 1940s was occupied by the Misses Evelyn and Nellie King and their sister Mrs Alderton. Their father was chaplain to the sisters at St Mary's Convent.

THE HARROW INN

The Harrow Inn, which stands on the junction of the Ridge and Maplehurst Road, was built in 1808. At one time there was a second hostelry at Baldslow, called the Hundreds Inn. The first registered owner of the Harrow Inn was Thomas Breeds and Company who no doubt replaced the resident tipple with his own locally brewed beer. The Harrow Inn was a landmark, not only for London stagecoaches but later as a stopping place for the local tram service. The spot achieved short-lived international fame when, sometime before WWI, possibly 1906, the balloon 'Banshee' made an emergency descent into the market garden of Mr Leslie Gower, a few yards from the inn. This event occurred during the James Gordon Bennett Paris to London balloon race. (It was this particular Gordon Bennett. who gave us the expletive). In 1936 the German Airship the Hindenburg passed over Baldslow. The well-known local family Webb held the license of the Harrow Inn for 50 years and they witnessed the change of brewer from Breeds to Gordon Beer and Rigden. In 1987 the Harrow Inn added a restaurant to the property, which is now part of the Brewer's Fayre chain.

ST MARY'S CONVENT, BALDSLOW

St Mary's Convent Baldslow, the residence of the Sisters of the Community of the Holy Family since 1913, is now converted into flats with houses in the grounds. The property estate is called by its original name; Holmhurst. Before it became a convent, the house was the home of the Reverend Augustus Hare, (1834-1903), who wrote ghost stories and topography and guide books, including one on Sussex, in which Hastings is featured. It was he who transported to the gardens at Holmhurst the statue of Queen Anne, where it remains to this day. The statue once stood in St Paul's Cathedral but was badly mutilated by a man, described according to different sources, as a lunatic or a drunken Lascar. The damaged monument was consigned to a stonemason's yard, where Hare discovered it and brought it to Hastings at the tremendous cost of £460.

Actress Miss Joanna Lumley, perhaps best remembered for her portrayals of Purdy in The Avengers and more recently, chain-smoking and champagne-swigging Patsy, in Absolutely Fabulous, was a pupil at St Mary's Convent from 1957. The convent's uniform, still remembered by older locals like me, was a saxe-blue overcoat and velour hat, a navy blue tunic, red and blue striped tie and grey socks. In her book, Stare Back and Smile, Miss Lumley gives an affectionate account of her years at St Mary's and a description of the house and grounds. Augustus Hare sold the house to the Community of the Holy Family on the condition that they kept intact his collection of natural history objects and continued to preserve the statue of Queen Anne in the grounds. Miss Lumley wrote that the house was a warren of wooden, gas-lit corridors, flanked by showcases containing Hare's collection; many of the corridors led to the girls' dormitories. These rooms were uncarpeted and unheated; in the winter, face flannels froze to the wash-bowl. The junior common room still had the original hand painted William Morris wallpaper, which the school-girl Joanna thought, 'rather dreadful'. She described the view of the garden: 'Wide windows looked over the terrace to the lawn on which the statue of Queen Anne crumbled, her hand holding the orb had fallen off and some of the seated figures had moulted pieces into the surrounding brambles'. There was a sloping sports field, a soft tennis court, colourful rhododendron shrubberies and a curved path that led past a lawn, a stagnant pond shaded by beech trees, flower and vegetable gardens and beyond, the nuns' graveyard. The regime was Anglo-Catholic but from Miss Lumley's account it seems that the school atmosphere was rather more relaxed than one might expect in a convent, giving an impression of a mixture of St Trinian's and the boarding schools in the 1930s stories by Angela Brazil but less resilient girls than Joanna may have seen the school differently. The boarders' spiritual needs were served in a chapel in the grounds and their trips to Hastings were rare; an orchestral concert at the White Rock or a visit to the indoor bathing pool. The school was surrounded by a high stone wall (some of which remains today) and a dense shrubbery, which excluded the outside world.

BEAULIEU FARM BALDSLOW

Mrs Enid Eldridge lives at Beaulieu Farm at Baldslow, (Beaulieu is pronounced Bowlew by locals), which has magnificent views over the countryside to Westfield, Guestling and far beyond. Beaulieu Farm was once part of the Beaulieu Estate, where stood Beaulieu House, demolished and rebuilt in the 1880s; later used as the boys' boarding school, Hydneye House. The farm stretches from Baldslow to Beaney's Lane; on an old but undated map the farm is marked as Windlands. The Eldridge family, who were tenant farmers at Nortons, Kent Street, Sedlescombe for 150 years, moved to Beaulieu Farm in 1926, becoming its owners in 1947. Enid's husband, Charles, born in 1927, was not only a farmer but an aspiring writer, with a strong feeling for the history of his district. He wrote "The Second Battle of Hastings", the story of an imaginary invasion on the Ridge by the Germans in 1940. Mr Eldridge died in 2004, shortly after the publication of his book. Mr and Mrs Eldridge's first home was at Yew Tree Cottage, The Ridge. (Yew Tree Cottage was owned by Mr Eldridge's grandmother Mrs Margaret King.) The cottage stands diagonally opposite to Lavender Cottage and Mrs Eldridge remembers seeing two elderly ladies pottering about its garden in the early 1950s, probably Emilie Crane and Clare Marriot but she did not speak to them as she said she was 'very shy'. Mrs Eldridge said that her wedding day was on October 28th 1950 and she confirmed that Emilie Crane's description of the weather in her letter of that time was correct; 'Icy, with frequent ground frosts, making gardening impossible'. The young Mr and Mrs Charles Eldridge eventually moved to live at Beaulieu Farm, where they brought up their four sons and two daughters. A Ridge road widening scheme brought about the demolition of the 400 year-old farmhouse in 1979 but Mr Eldridge insisted on carefully dismantling the property himself. A group of historical architects were on hand to note the details of the ancient building for their archive.

Mr Eldridge salvaged the former farmhouse porch, along with its door and flooring, where his wife's initials and the date 1950 are impressed on the threshold. The porch now forms a unique garden loggia, which is crammed with grandchildren's outdoor playthings. For sentimental reasons Mr Charles Eldridge also rescued the little wooden, tile-hung steeple of St Luke's Church, Silverhill, which was toppled in the 1987

The 400 year old Beaulieu Farmhouse, demolished 1979.

St Peter's Church Baldslow,
demolished 1979.

The entrance to St Mary's Convent School for Girls.

Baldslow Mill, after conversion to a house.

St Peter's Church outing

St Peter's Harvest Festival

hurricane. Charles' great-grandfather was a founder member of the church in 1853 and the Eldridges have worshipped there since then. Apart from a two year break a member of the family has been an office bearer at the church for the past 150 years. No wonder then that the steeple was a precious relic to the family. Single handedly, Charles Eldridge erected it in his garden at Beaulieu Farm, where it now stands among the flowerbeds of the re-built farmhouse. The Eldridge's working and social life was inevitably involved with their immediate surroundings. Mrs Eldridge formed friendships with the sisters of the convent at Holmhurst St Mary's Anglican Convent, immediately opposite the farm and she used the shops at nearby Baldslow Village for her daily needs. Beaulieu Dairy Farm delivered their own milk twice a day at one time, originally to Baldslow and the Westfield Lane area. Mrs Eldridge's sons remembered delivering milk from the farm to the very elderly Mrs Todd, Emilie Crane's neighbour, friend and eventually her cleaning lady. Charles Eldridge formed the Beaulieu Cricket Team in 1943 and they played on one of the farm's fields, close to the Ridge. The team, still in existence, moved to William Parker School's practice grounds in the early 1990s, bowing to the modern demand for changing rooms and hot showers. With six schools still situated on the Ridge in the 1950s, there were sports fields to be maintained and Mr Eldridge gang-mowed the grass at Hydeneye House, St Margaret's School, St Mary's, Claremont School and Glengorse School and many other local football and recreational fields. The former East Lodge of Hydneye is occupied by one of the Eldridge sons, Christopher, and his brother Robert, known as Will, runs an agricultural machinery business from the site. Mrs Eldridge commented on the rural appearance of the Ridge in the 1950s. She often walked between Yew Tree Cottage and Beaulieu Farm, with her baby son in the pram, taking to the middle of the road, as there was no proper pavement and passing traffic was infrequent.

ST PETER'S CHURCH

Also demolished under the Ridge new road scheme was St Peter's Church, a Victorian, corrugated iron chapel that stood close by the farm house. Mr Eldridge took photographs of this demolition and saved the chapel bell, which is now suspended under the wood and glass cupola that once formed part of the roof of the Beaulieu Farmhouse dairy. When the rope is pulled the old church bell issues a discordant 'clang' that seems to befit an iron church. Mrs Eldridge recalled seeing the boys from Hydeneye House going to St Peter's Church, called the 'Tin Tabernacle' by locals. The boys walked in a crocodile, dressed in uniform red caps and blazers. The actual date of the beginning of St Peter's Church is difficult to pin-point from the rather vague records that exist but it is believed it was built early in 1863, under the auspices of Mr E Habershon, an architect and the owner of Beaulieu House. The simple church had a schoolroom attached, which was used as a Sunday school. One of the worshippers was the Reverend Augustus Hare, from Holmhurst, the house opposite to St Peters. There was a brass plaque in the church, commemorating those who died in the 1914-1918 war, bearing the names: George Baker, Charles Cole (son of the Vicar; the family lived in Upper Glen Road and his sister Bessie ran a small school), Norman E. Dawson, Ernest Drury, George Gray, Eric Penn, Ernest Scotcher, George Scotcher, Reginald Stevens and Charles West. Mr Pat Held was a member of St Peter's congregation in his youth and he provided the two photographs in this book of church activities from the late sixties/early seventies. One picture shows the interior of the church dressed for a harvest festival, the pews garlanded with late summer flowers and baskets of produce laid at the altar. The minister in the picture is locum, The Rev. Godfrey. The other is a snap taken on a church outing. In the centre of the picture in the cloche hat is Miss Cole: She was the daughter of the Reverend Cole, once minister at St Peter's. Miss Cole was a formidable lady according to Pat Held, who was her nephew. He said that she was a powerful force in the church, the Superintendent of the Sunday school and the organiser of other activities, such as the sale of work. He continued: 'The church outings were quite simple affairs in those days; a trip to Drusilla's - the children's zoo, or to the Wannock Gardens Tea Rooms, at Eastbourne but we looked forward to them and found the trips enjoyable.' Pat Held can be seen at the extreme right of the picture, bearing two ice creams; his fiancée, Mary Finch, later his wife, is to the right of Miss Cole.

HYDNEYE HOUSE PREPARATORY SCHOOL FOR BOYS

Hydneye House Preparatory School for Boys previously occupied the land on which Helenswood Lower School now stands. Hydeneye House was designed by Ernest Pilkington and constructed in stages between 1870 and 1890. Italian craftsmen living at Baldslow painted and gilded one room, created magnificent moulded ceilings and panelled the walls with oak; even the stables featured terracotta decorations. The building was used as a boys' preparatory boarding and day school from 1918.

The origins of the school are noted in the Hydneye House School Magazine of March 1957: "Hydneye House was a name given to a school founded in about 1900 at Willingdon, near Eastbourne by Mr Norman. In 1911 he was joined by Mr J R W Tanner. There were not many boys in these days, but by 1914 the numbers had risen to 35 and in this year, Mr E G Maltby joined the school. As there was no room for further expansion in the house at Willingdon, a search was made for other premises and in September 1918, Hydneye House moved to its present quarters at Baldslow, to a house then called Beaulieu. Soon after the arrival at Baldslow new dormitories were built on over the West Wing and the pupil numbers rose to sixty. In 1923 Mr Tanner retired from the school but his brother Mr O C R Tanner had joined it, as also had Mr E P K Hough, who was to die tragically just before the war. With the move to Hastings the school began to flourish and rapidly became one of the best known schools in the district, especially in its games record. When the war came in 1939, the school evacuated to Devon. The army occupied Hydneye during the war and when the school returned afterwards much had to be done to put the house and grounds back in order. Mr O C R Tanner had become a partner, and in 1950 Mr A F Bassett became the third member of the partnership. At the end of the winter term 1955 Mr Tanner retired and at the end of the next term Mr and Mrs Maltby retired, after having been connected with the school for over forty years. The Maltbys had a son, David, who was born in the cottage at Hydneye. In WWII David was one of the RAF Dambusters; he survived that operation but was killed soon after, aged 28. Mr Maltby's successor was Headmaster, Mr Gerald Brodribb, an old boy of the school whose family had been connected with Hydneye since 1918. Mr Bassett remained on as a partner" The history concludes, "Perhaps one of these days, an expedition can be made to the long forgotten landing place of Hyd-n-eye, the ancient harbour island in the marsh. The sea-waters may have come and gone, but the present school has risen Phoenix-like from those Celtic ashes. May the name of Hydneye flourish for ever on the crest of those waves." The new dormitories mentioned were built by Henry Ransom; care was taken that the extension should merge with and preserve the character of Pilkington's original design. In about 1919 the stables were converted for accommodation for domestic staff and further dormitories, a carpenter's shop for woodwork classes, a garage and a gymnasium were added. In 1920 a bridge was constructed to link the stable block to the main building; the bridge was built of red brick and tile, to mimic the style of the main building.

Headmaster Gerald Brodribb came to wider public attention as a result of discovering clues that led to the unearthing of extensive Roman iron workings and bath site, hidden for centuries under a slag heap in the 900 acres of woodland at Beauport Park, not far from Hydneye House. The second century site, dated about 250AD, has been described as probably the largest of its kind in Europe. It was first uncovered in 1973 but kept secret for more than 10 years. Brodribb originally worked alone on the site but was later joined by John Manwaring Baines, the curator of Hastings Museum. Early excavations had revealed sections of walls standing to a height of three feet and 2000 tiles were also found on the site; these were stamped CLB-Classis Britannica, which suggests that the site was a fitting-out depot for the Roman Navy. In his retirement Brodribb discussed his Roman discoveries on the TV programme, Time Team with presenter Tony Robinson, who, some thought, interviewed Brodribb in an unnecessarily challenging manner. The site was in-filled to protect it from vandals and weather; it was Brodribb's hope that the responsibility for this valuable archaeological discovery would be taken on by English Heritage, a hope that was not fulfilled at the time of his death in October 1999. Gerald Brodribb, kept in touch with his former pupils and would invite them back to the school to form a team, to play cricket against the Hydneye House boys. Brodribb, famous in his own right as a prolific cricket writer, (one of his best-known cricket books was 'Felix on the Bat'), claimed a family link with the Victorian actor Sir Henry Irving, whose real name was John Brodribb. There has

Little Ridge Farm, now the Conquest Hospital site.

German Plane crash at Beaney's Lane, 1940

Hydneye House School.

Hydneye House School yard. c.1963

been an unsubstantiated reference to a science master at Hydneye, Mr Miller, supposedly being John Logie Baird's assistant, when he invented television in Hastings.

Former Hydneye House boy, James Barnes-Phillips, came to my attention in an article in the Hastings and St Leonards Observer of January 2004. He had organised a get-together of Hydneye old boys. James provided me with the short history of the school and a collection of emailed memories from fellow pupils who were at the school from the early and mid-1960s. Apart from references to listening to pop music on a transistor radio hidden under the bed sheets, the memories could have been taken from the daily life of a preparatory school of any period in the previous four or five decades. Discretion forbids details but there were rumours of dalliances between the resident teaching and domestic staff and recollections of crushes that the boys harboured for the young assistant matrons, in two cases these were girls who had been pupils at St Mary's Convent boarding school, which was set a tantalizing few hundred yards from Hydneye House. Many ex-pupils conjectured how the school's regime would have measured up against today's politically correct criteria, as far as discipline and staff conduct were concerned. However, it's certain Hydneye House was not alone in this.

Respected or disliked teachers are mentioned by name in the recollections; most boys of the period will recall Mr Hilder, teacher of history and geography with a fiery temper, who was nicknamed Volcano. He was a keen cricketer and therefore accurate in 'scoring', when he threw the blackboard rubber, a chunk of wood with a thin felt covering, at any boy who misbehaved. Boarder, Bill Moseley, later well known as the owner of the Hastings Town Centre Ironmongery store, has, however, good memories of Mr Hilder for the cricket skills he taught him, especially during the Easter holidays, when locally-resident boys were invited into the school to learn how to coach, for the coming cricket season. Bill said that punishment for misdemeanors in school was swift and no quarter was given to new boys. In his first few days at the school the boys in his dormitory used the hollow metal frames of their army-type beds to compress and squirt the contents of tubes of toothpaste all over the room; every boy, including Bill, was given four strokes of the gym slipper. However Bill said he enjoyed his time at Hydneye, where he stayed until he was eleven years old. Remembered with fondness by another old boy is the woodwork teacher, 'I am grateful to him to this day for the basic DIY skills he instilled in me'. Patrick Moore made several visit to the school to talk about astronomy and Hastings Chess Congress contestants played matches with the boys. Midnight feasts, a roaming boy sleep-walker, the queue at the tuck shop and sports events, especially cricket feature prominently in the boys' memories, as do the nicknames and peculiarities of their contemporaries.

The boys of Hydneye House built an amphitheatre in the school grounds. One ex-pupil, nicknamed Mr Secretary, said: 'I remember at the end of one term, student actors from Balliol College Oxford (the Balliol Players) came to give a show in the amphitheatre. They probably performed something of an improving nature, but all I can remember is their stunning, a Capella renditions of the Everley Brothers' 'Bird Dog' and Elvis' 'Good Luck Charm'.

Several boys mentioned attending Sunday morning service at St Peter's Baldslow, or 'little house on the prairie' as one called it, sometimes accompanied by their parents who were visiting for the weekend. One minister who had a long droopy Edwardian moustache was dubbed Father Christmas by the boys. Sadly, Hydneye House School did not 'flourish for ever'. It was obtained by a compulsory purchase order; the intention to carry out the order was unexpectedly revealed by Hastings Borough Council in 1968. Brodribb claimed at the time, 'It has come as a complete shock to me that there is a proposal for a new secondary school to be built on the site of Hydneye House and the information will damage the business prospects of the school'. From the date of the proposal becoming known not one new boy was entered for the school, which closed in 1969. When Bill Moseley paid a nostalgic visit to the site the contractors demolishing the building told him that they had found 2,500 glass marbles and a collection of penknives under the floor-grills, which covered the central heating pipes. Ex-pupils who made visits to the Hydneye grounds in the late 1970s found only the swimming pool and the amphitheatre remaining; another visitor took away one of the grey bricks that formerly surfaced the yard, where the boys once played football. On its closure Hydneye House merged with Glengorse

Preparatory School in Battle to form 'Glengorse and Hydneye Preparatory School'. This in turn merged with Battle Abbey School in 1989. The new Helenswood Lower School was opened in November 1979.

LITTLE RIDGE FARM

The land on which Little Ridge Farm stood was once known as the Parish of St Mary in the Castle, which extended some way north of the Ridge. The land was a tenement of the joint Manor of Etchingham and Salehurst, along with Windlands, now Beaulieu Farm. Little Ridge incorporated Great Ridge Farm in the old Parish of Ore. Records from 1658 show that Little Ridge Farm consisted of houses and 80 acres of land; the farm is known to have existed in the 16th century. In 1860 the estate was purchased by Maria Hare the adoptive mother of Rev.Augustus Hare. It is presumed the Hares let the farm or sold it off. The Old Roar Stream rises from two ponds in the area, one in the ground of St Mary's and the other in the home yard of the farm. The waters have formed a ravine which culminates in a waterfall known as Old Roar Ghyll, to be found at the north end of Hastings' Alexandra Park. In 1992 the Conquest Hospital was built on Little Ridge Farm and only the farmhouse and small area of yard still exists. At the rear of the hospital there is a lake, described on the official prospectus as a 'lagoon', but this is not shown on old maps. It appears the lagoon was previously a dry hollow, probably a quarry for clay or stone; where cattle would graze. There was a second, similarly-shaped depression on the farm and an area called Quarry Field. The land behind the former Avondale Laundry, which stood about 500 yards along the road from the farm, was called the brickfield. There is a sand quarry and other sites at Baldslow from which stone was hewed. This now almost forgotten industry no doubt supplied the demand for building materials in the surges of development in Hastings and St Leonards in the 18th and 19th centuries. Holford Pitcher was the last man to work Little Ridge Farm before it disappeared under the hospital. His mother believed that the farmhouse was haunted by the spirit of a young, distressed girl, who would stand at the foot of her bed. Apparently, Mrs Pitcher was unafraid of the phantom and would say to it. 'It's alright dear'. Holford said he had not seen this manifestation but was aware of an eerie atmosphere in a narrow passageway by the farmhouse fireplace. A previous occupant of the farm had mentioned what sounds like poltergeist activity, with shards of glass being thrown down the stairs by an invisible force. Holford also said that there had been a suicide at the farm in its recent history. When his family took over the farm in the late 1950s, townspeople who came to buy eggs would refer the Ridge as 'the country', which Holford thought strange, as the Pitchers had moved in from the very rural area beyond Battle. Holford said the farmhouse was very damp and after the property was sold builders found that the foundations of the house were filled with standing water.

LANDSVIEW TERRACE

Mrs Carey, who lives in Landsview Terrace, close to Little Ridge Farm House, moved to Hastings from Suffolk in WWII, after she had joined the Auxiliary Training Service. She was stationed on the Ridge, at Coghurst Hall, which was commandeered by the army, as were most of the larger establishments in the area. Mrs Carey was an ATS cook and catered for 50 to 60 people on the Aga cooker in the Coghurst Hall kitchen. The majority of the resident ATS women were taken by army truck to Ore Place, where they did military clerical work. Mrs Carey remembers Coghurst Hall and the gardens as beautiful and peaceful, apart from the time that the building suffered German machine-gunning. During her time at Coghurst she was taken ill and she had to sleep in the sickbay at Hurst Court, also commandeered by the army. After the war, Mrs Carey married a Hastings man, whose father had worked in the gardens of Coghurst Hall and his mother was employed in the house. The young Careys went to live at the Ridge address in 1947, where Mrs Carey still resides. Mrs Carey remembers Mrs Todd, a former neighbour and the owner of Laura, the parrot, who both appear in Letters from Lavender Cottage. She knew nothing of the parrot but recalls Mrs Todd as a person who was forthright and spoke her mind but tended to look on the black side of life; her sombre style of dress reflected her personality. This confirms Emilie Crane's opinion of Mrs Todd as 'somewhat mournful'. Mrs Carey worshipped at St Helen's Church, on the Ridge, for many years and she used to attend the open air services in the ruins of the ancient St Helen's Church. She said that wooden pews and a harmonium were carried across the field to the old church and it never seemed to rain on that special day. Mrs Carey recalled going to Hydeneye House School for Boys for celebrations for VE Day and that a screen was set up in a hall there, so that a film could be shown to the party.

AVONDALE LAUNDRY.

Tim Tidmarsh was born in 1949 in the former Avondale Laundry, (now demolished) at 447 the Ridge, where he lived with his two sisters Jennie and Elizabeth. The family had bought the premises in 1945/46 and converted the laundry into a house, which they named Willowdene. Tim's mother, Joan was very much involved with the life of St Helen's church and became the superintendent of its Sunday school. Tim's grandfather, George Allen was a gardener and he undertook to maintain about 250 graves in Hastings Cemetery. Tim thinks that the fee for this work was 2 guineas (£2.10p) a year, per grave. Tim's other grandfather, Charles Redhead, took on the business of caring for some of the graves after George's death. This work passed to his daughter Joan and as a small child Tim would accompany her in the cemetery and he learned to read from the large letters on the tombstone inscriptions. Charles Redhead was a keen gardener and one of the highlights of his year was the flower show, held in the field behind St Helen's Church. There would be a marquee set up; side shows, hoop-la and bowling for a pig.

When Tim was growing up, children tended to keep very much to their own patch and his stretched from Little Ridge Farm to St Helen's Church, taking in the surrounding fields, woods and lanes, many of which were still unmade tracks. He recalls that as a child he hardly ever ventured the half-mile into Baldslow Village. At the age of about thirteen Tim took on pocket money jobs; he delivered newspapers to nearby homes and farms for local newsagent, Mr McKinley and helped out at Little Ridge Farm. Tim had only faint memories of the Avondale Laundry in business. He said that they did the laundry of St Margaret's Boarding School for Girls and there were two long, shed-like rooms where women would stand, hand-ironing sheets and linens all day. As a boy Tim went carol-singing round the large houses in the locality and would get glimpses into homes that hinted at wealth and comfort. He remembered most particularly looking inside the large entrance hall of a house called Quarry Wood and seeing a huge stuffed dog and on a wall a picture that seemed to him to be many feet high and wide, depicting Highland cattle. It may well be, however, that the impression of wealth in these families was more illusory than real, bearing in mind how quickly many of the houses and their grounds were sold off for development on the death of their owners. Quarry Wood was occupied by Miss Alder and Miss Brooks. Tim also knew the Pitcairn-Knowles family, who ran the Riposo Nature Cure Hydro, very close to his home. When I showed him the photograph of the hydrotherapy treatment room at Riposo he said that he remembered seeing the hip baths, discarded in the garden, when the premises were under demolition. Tim remembered Mrs Todd, who owned the parrot Laura, so frequently mentioned in Emilie Crane's letters from Lavender Cottage. He used to see Mrs Todd going along to the little stores near Lavender Cottage; she was dressed in a long dark coat like a clergyman's and carried a wicker basket. Mrs Todd would buy just one item, only to return to the shop soon after to buy another. Tim described her as being of a mournful demeanor. He said he had heard the squawking of Mrs Todd's parrot, when it was put out in the garden for an airing.

RIPOSO NATURE CURE HEALTH HYDRO.

The Riposo Nature Cure Hydro on the Ridge was founded by Andrew Pitcairn-Knowles in 1913. Prior to undertaking this venture, he had been a keen sportsman and a pioneer photo-journalist. As the 20th Century opened he was living in Berlin and was the editor of two German language sporting magazines, Sport im Bild the first-ever illustrated magazines devoted to sport and Sport im Wort. Pitcairn-Knowles subsequently toured Europe for 10 years with his family, writing articles and taking hundreds of photographs to illustrate his articles for British and Continental magazines. It was during this tour that a serious accident occurred to his son Gordon, an event which heralded a turning point in the family's life. At six years old, Gordon was kicked in the stomach by a mule, which injured him severely and led to a deteriorating condition. Despairing of conventional treatments, the family returned to Germany and the Nature Cure system of Doctor Spohr. Impressed by the child's improvement in health under this system, Andrew set aside his photo-journalism career and toured the

Riposo Nature Cure Hydro.

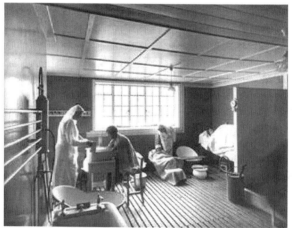

Hydrotherapy treatment at Riposo.

Riposo. Patient's Chalet.

Chalet Interior.

Oakhurst Hotel.

Netherwood Guesthouse

The Grange School for Boys.

Yew Tree Cottage.

spas and health hydros of Europe, studying their methods. Andrew and his wife, Margaret, decided to open the first English nature cure health hydro so they bought a large house in Hastings, called Ridgecroft, on the Ridge and re-named it Riposo. With a war looming it was not the most propitious time to be founding an enterprise based on revolutionary principles. In spite of the difficulties created by the war, Riposo was established and was able to expand after hostilities ended in 1918. Gordon Pitcairn-Knowles had almost died from influenza whilst serving in the Royal Navy but once again, nature cure saved his life. In his early twenties Gordon studied his father's methods and attained membership of the Nature Cure Association and joined his parents in running Riposo for the next 40 years.

The bigger bedrooms in Riposo were divided to make more sleeping accommodation, with staff housed in the four attic bedrooms. Over the years the grounds were developed with about 30, double-walled wooden chalets, some placed in separate enclosures for women or men. The chalets had gas lighting and fires and were very cosy, even in winter and every day staff had to carry hot water to each chalet occupant, as well as meals for bed patients. The last two chalets, built in 1930, had electric light. The dietary regime of the establishment was lacto-vegetarian coupled with water treatments and fasts. There was a large kitchen in the main house; Nellie Rothan was the cook, assisted by her sister Beattie; Harry Constantine was the waiter. Harry was something of an artist and made a painting from a photograph of Riposo that was printed as a postcard; he went on to do this work full-time for the Hastings firm, Judges Postcards. He had an etching exhibited at the Royal Academy Exhibition in 1961 (No 1169).

The 'goings on' at Riposo were a matter of some interest to locals; vegetarianism and nature cures were little understood at that time and their devotees were seen as cranks and eccentrics. There was gossip of the Riposo patients rolling naked in the dew, as part of their therapy and small and not so small boys attempted to get a clandestine view. Local lads would make sure to be on the upper deck of the trolley bus that passed Riposo, in the hope of seeing the 'nudists'. Certainly, patients were encouraged to walk barefoot in the dew and nude sunbathing was permitted in the privacy of the chalet enclosures. The hydro also provided a social life, with garden parties, car treasure hunts and picnics to entertain the patients. In the summer seasons, at the height of its popularity Riposo could have as many as 50 patients. For the Pitcairn-Knowles family their healing work provided an idealistic life. In 1929 Gordon married Joyce, who had come to work at the hydro as the secretary. Their son, Richard, was born in 1932 in their home in the stable- block cottage at Riposo. The declaration of WWII must have come as particularly painful news to Richard's family, who had many friends in Germany, dating from his grandfather's career and residence in Berlin, well before the Great War. Wartime food rationing did not seem to make much impact on the Riposo ménage; as they were lacto-vegetarians. In place of meat they received a slightly increased cheese ration and 'Digging for Victory' in the gardens and keeping hens provided plenty of vegetables, fruit and eggs. Coal and coke were also rationed and hot water was essential to hydrotherapy. However, the war had reduced the number of patients so the supplies of fuel never quite ran out.

After the war, Gordon Pitcairn-Knowles began to renovate Riposo, a task that turned into a continuing struggle. His 76 year-old father, who died in 1956, found it difficult to hand over the control of his own creation, which he had kept going through two world wars. By the 1950s Gordon was running Riposo but still found time to give talks about natural healing methods at the White Rock Pavilion to the Vegetarian Society and to other groups. Gordon Pitcairn-Knowles died in 1963 aged 62. Riposo and its grounds were sold for development but the legacy of healing continues with Andrew Pitcairn-Knowles' descendents, who work in the fields of osteopathy, naturopathy, speech and occupational therapy and fitness instruction. The Andrew Pitcairn-Knowles archive of documents and pre-1914 photographs is now housed at the Victoria and Albert Museum. I am left wondering if Emilie Crane and her Lavender Cottage friends knew the Pitcairn-Knowles family. Certainly they were among the 'nice folk around here', of whom Emilie writes in her letters.

YEW TREE COTTAGE

The history of the cottage is rather vague; it has been suggested that it was once the lodge gatehouse of the Grange. Alternatively, it was built in the early 18th century and was one of the several turnpike cottages along what was then the London Road and there is some connection with smugglers. One informant said that Mr Clayton, the inventor of the warmed toilet seat, once lived at Yew Tree Cottage.

THE RIDGE SHOPS

A few yards east of Lavender Cottage there were two shops: one owned by Watson the Grocer, to whom there are several references in this book and McKinley the newsagent. In Emilie Crane's early years on the Ridge the newsagent was owned by Mr Rowe, whose son, Lyndon became a bus enthusiast. Lyndon W Rowe wrote in his book, Hastings Trolleybuses, of living above his father's shop on the Ridge: "Perhaps it was the shadow of the trolley booms across my bedroom ceiling at night, as a Guy single-decker passed by on the infrequent, circular Ridge route that gave me a love for the system and ensured that I was present on 31st May 1959 to see the very last trolleybus to pass my birthplace and pre-war, former home". It is clear from her letters that Emilie Crane and her friends made use of the trolleybus service that passed their house and thanks to Lyndon Rowe we have an account of an image Emilie must have seen from the front rooms of the cottage. When the Lavender Cottage occupants first took up residence (1929/1930) the Ridge route was serviced by a variety of public vehicles, as it was a period of change-over. The open topped and the Guy single-decker trolley buses shared the route with the new double-decker trolleybus. Some of the single-deckers were of a very old type and had oil lamps as interior lighting and headlights, which were sometimes extinguished during a journey by the Ridge's strong winds. Next to the shops, at 400 The Ridge is Scollays, one of the few remaining old families still in business on the Ridge, running a garden supply and hardware store.

OAKHURST HOTEL.

From the age of 16 in 1962, Roger Tilbury lived at the Oakhurst Hotel, which stood among trees near the entrance to Grange Road, on the Ridge. The hotel was at one time in the joint ownership of Roger's uncle, Richard Underwood and Vernon Symonds and they also jointly owned Netherwood, a guest house that was set in the same area of spacious grounds and woodland. (See map.) Sometime in the 1950s Richard Underwood ended the shared ownership arrangement and he took over sole ownership of Oakhurst, turning it into an hotel, which he ran with Roger's parents, Ted and Joan, who had joined him in 1962. Richard married Irene in 1958 and they all undertook to manage the hotel together. From the Oakhurst Hotel brochure and Roger's anecdotes we get an impression of a comfortable and informal establishment. I said to Roger that I gathered from his stories that there was a hint of 'Fawlty Towers' about Oakhurst; he agreed that it was true to some extent -in nice way, but added that his father was not at all like Basil Fawlty!

The hotel was staffed by local women, on a part-time basis, with the help of students on holiday in the summer season. Oakhurst had its share of amusing incidents and characters. In 1964-65 Mayor Douglas William Wilshin came to dinner; Carol, a waitress who was the hotel's only professional staff member, was chosen to serve this important guest but she managed to empty the mayor's dinner into his lap. On another occasion waitress June tripped and hurled a tray of servings of tomato soups at the wall; (shades of Acorn Antiques!) Roger said that at one time the hotel hosted left-wing conferences at winter weekends, mainly because his Uncle Richard was somewhat pink in his politics but when prices were increased the delegates stopped coming. Early in his career, Welshman Clive Jenkins was at the hotel a couple of times, with what was then a fledgling trade union. Mr Jenkins became the general secretary of the white-collar union, the Association of Scientific, Technical and Managerial Staffs, a position he held for about 20 years. He was regarded as something of a champagne socialist and his witty and stylish speeches delighted or enraged listeners, according to their politics. Roger remembered an occurrence at the hotel that had a nice 'socialist' touch: 'Some guests, who were a very working-class family from Newcastle, were unable to book a taxi to catch the first train of the morning. Staying at the hotel at the same time was Mr Warwick-Haller, solicitor to half of Hampshire, whose daughter was a boarder at Holmhurst St Mary's School at Baldslow. Her parents travelled to Hastings to visit their daughter in either one of their two Rollers, a Bentley and, once to our astonishment, an Austin A40. Mr Warwick-Haller said to the stranded family, 'I always get up early; I'll run you down to the station'. He did - in the large Rolls'.

Other guests Roger remembers were two well known men, Owen

Hindle and Peter Clarke, players who had come to town to participate in the Hastings Chess Congress. There was an old Eastbourne bus in the grounds behind Oakhurst and in the late 1950s it was home to two struggling folk-singers. They were Shirley and Dolly Collins, sisters born in the Hastings area, who used local and traditional music as a basis for their compositions and performances. They subsequently made many records and still have a considerable following on the national and international folk scene. A famous neighbour was Alfie Bass, the cockney character film and television actor, perhaps best remembered for his role as the sore-footed 'Bootsie' in the TV series, The Army Game. He bought a small-holding-cum holiday home in a lane near the Oakhurst Hotel and would call there to borrow sugar or coffee or whatever he had run out of. Actor Bill Fraser, Alfie's side kick in The Army Game, was also a frequent visitor to Hastings at that time. Roger continued: 'Many families came back year after year; we had four acres of grounds which provided putting, lawn tennis, table tennis, croquet, badminton, a sandpit and paddling pool and a lawn large enough for tennis-ball cricket. At least one family, having seen all the sights on their first visit, spent the whole fortnight in the following years in the grounds of the hotel. My father used to greet new people and surprise them by identifying the home town of most of them. He knew the car registration letters and so, if we only had one family booked in from, for example, St Alban's, it was a fair bet that they had a car with that registration. My father always signed hotel letters as 'Ted Tilbury'. The postman once correctly delivered a letter addressed to Ted Hotel, Hastings, Sussex'.

The hotel had a few long-term guests; Roger remembers H.B Cox, who was Colonel-in-Charge at Ore Place, on the Ridge, the Army Records Office. Roger said: 'He stayed with us for three years. He was a most unlikely colonel. He invented indoor ice-hockey on the parquet floor of the lounge with a kid's plastic hockey sticks and a weighted matchbox. At first we were a bit in awe of him but when the summer was over and he became the only guest, he wandered into the kitchen one morning and asked if he could have his breakfast there with us, as it was a bit lonely all by himself in the dining room. Another time in the winter of 1962-63 there had been heavy snow and we couldn't find the colonel. He was clearing the 50 yard drive because he liked shovelling snow. One day the drive was so frozen that my Aunt Irene couldn't move the car from the front door to the garage. Colonel Cox got in and drove it round to the garage first time - to my aunt's displeasure. One weekend, a conference cancelled at the last minute so there were 48 lamb chops in the freezer; the colonel came into the kitchen to find me chiselling his steak off the chops. In the winter there was only the odd guest to join the colonel and another long-term resident, Mr Butler, who managed the electronics factory in the Ridge's Woodlands Way. We served them dinner at a big foldaway table in the corner of the lounge. One evening we were a bit behind so I hurriedly wheeled in a trolley with the necessities to lay the table. I took the 90 degree corner into the lounge just a tad too fast and shot a bottle of ketchup off the side of the trolley. The bottle fell from the trolley onto the black and white tiled floor, smashed and splashed scarlet over the pale blue wrought iron grill that was underneath the notice board. Uttering appropriate curses, I put the trolley in the lounge and went for broom, mop and bucket. In my brief absence two elderly ladies came down the stairs. No, they were not permanent residents; their names were not Miss Tibbs and Miss Gatsby (of Fawlty Tower's fame). On seeing the red-splattered wreckage one of the ladies fainted and the other was not much better. Mr Butler was nearly as much of a character as the colonel. He was a freemason, among various other things. One evening, he decided at dinner that he and I would go to see the wrestling matches at the White Rock Pavilion. I hoped it wouldn't be too expensive but we went straight in, down the aisle and up the steps to the stage and sat down at the ringside. When we watched the Sussex team play at the old Central Cricket Ground it was from the pavilion. He never seemed to pay for any of these privileges. He'd been a destroyer captain in WWII: They had captured a German U-Boat and taken the crew off the vessel before they sank it. The U-Boat commander believed that the British Navy sank enemy submarines along with the crew and was so grateful to be wrong that he gave Captain Butler his Zeiss night binoculars.

I remember the heavy snow of 1962-63 that started on Boxing Day; several guests were obliged to stay longer than they planned. I tried to get to London to see my girlfriend on the 27th December but gave up, after four hours of waiting at Tonbridge and got a train back, which took another three hours. Then the number 75 bus could only get as far as the Pilot Field and I had to struggle up the rest of Elphinstone Road as best I could. Christmas at Oakhurst was always great fun. We had our own family Christmas celebrations at New Year, when we were closed for business. The hotel Christmas Day began at six in the morning, with the cleaning. We always had a full kitchen staff but sometimes, despite paying triple wages of twelve shillings an hour (60p), we were a little short-staffed for other duties. There was breakfast to prepare and wash-up; morning coffee to be served and lunch to be laid. Then came the washing up, which staff member Kathy and I always did. We used almost boiling water with a soapy sink and a clean sink. That way everything dried in the racks, obviating the need for drying. It was the one day we served wine - a ghastly cheap Sauternes. Kathy and I used to finish off the left-over wine as we worked. The scullery floor would be under an inch or two of water but the washing up got done in record time. We also served afternoon tea and a buffet evening meal. As soon as that was cleared away and washed up the evening games and dancing had to be organised and compered - with tea and biscuits served at 10.00pm. We got to bed around two in the morning, only to start a repeat performance at 6.00am on Boxing Day.

People seemed to be able to eat in those days without getting obese. One very wet August Bank holiday, everyone was indoors and bored; we wheeled in the first trolley with the food on it and people helped themselves, while we went for the tea trolley. In under a minute the first trolley was stripped bare and there was a queue waiting for further supplies. That was the Bank Holiday that Tim O'Donoghue and his ten-year old daughter, previous guests of the hotel, turned up on the Saturday evening, wanting a bed. We pointed out we had no beds available; even the two caravans we kept in the grounds and the annex flat across the road were full. 'But, surely, there must be somewhere, said Tim? To put him off, father offered two camp beds in the garage. And Tim responded' 'And what more could a man and child be wanting than that?' So they slept a couple of nights on camp beds in the garage!'

Roger concluded; 'Despite the occasional resemblance to a certain fictitious establishment in Torquay, Oakhurst Hotel hardly ever had to advertise. Ninety per cent of guests were returns or recommendations. In 1968 Oakhurst was sold for a new housing development.'

NETHERWOOD GUEST HOUSE

Netherwood Guest House on the Ridge was at one period owned by Kathleen, (known as Johnny) and Vernon Symonds. Netherwood was a gabled, Victorian property, standing in four acres of grounds, with outbuildings, gardens, a grass tennis court, shrubberies and tall trees. An 1873 Ordnance Survey map names the place as Western House but on the OS map of 1899 it is shown as Netherwood. The Symonds managed to keep the guest house running after a fashion during WWII, with a few guests, in spite of Hastings' restricted area status keeping visitors from the town. About half a mile from Netherwood, in Grange Road, was an army camp based in and around the Grange School for Boys, which the army had commandeered for the duration. It was also used to contain German and Italian prisoners of war. The soldiers and ATS women stationed at the army camp used Netherwood as a canteen and an informal club house and the Symonds were allocated extra rations to provide snacks for them, as well as serving lunches to the military and civilian administration staff at nearby Ore Place. Vernon Symonds, who was keen on amateur dramatics, had performed with Hastings Court Players and he assisted in the founding of Hastings' Stables Theatre. In the late 1940s and 1950s, Netherwood was a popular venue for trade union and political gatherings and regarded by locals as a left-wing haven. Vernon Symonds had contacts with figures in the worlds of politics, the arts and sciences, which enabled him to invite luminaries to Netherwood on the understanding that in return for bed and board they gave a talk on their ideas and work to the other guests. Among famous visitors were Edith Bone, Professor C.E.M. Joad, J.B.S. Haldane, Professor Jacob Bronowski and Harry Pollitt.

Professor C.E.M. Joad was a civil servant, later head of the philosophy department at Birkbeck College, London. He wrote many books but is generally best remembered for his appearances on the BBC radio programme, The Brains Trust and for his habit of prefacing his replies to listeners' questions with, "It all depends on what you mean by..."

J.B.S. Haldane was descended from Scottish aristocrats. Educated at Eton and Oxford, he became a socialist after service in the trenches as an officer in the First World War. He aimed to bring an understanding of science to the masses. Doctor Edith Bone was a Hungarian aristocrat and medical professor, married to a British National. She was a foreign correspondent for the Daily Worker and from 1949 was imprisoned by the Hungarian Communist authorities and kept in solitary confinement for seven years, without trial. Jacob Bronowski was Polish-born, a mathematician and physicist, a brilliant thinker and an inspiring and excitable speaker. He also appeared on the Brains Trust but is best remembered for his mid-1970s TV programe, The Ascent of Man. Harry Pollitt was the General Secretary and Chairman of the Communist Party of Great Britain.

Netherwood was also home to Aleister Crowley for the last two years of his life. He was internationally infamous as an occultist, who practiced what he termed 'magick', which had unsavoury sexual overtones. He was self-styled 'the Great Beast, 666'. At the end of the war, Crowley was lodging in uncomfortable digs in Surrey and his already poor health had deteriorated. Lois Wilkinson, an old friend of Crowley, had heard about Netherwood and its eccentric owners and he asked if the Symonds would be prepared to take in such an ill-famed guest. Crowley, aged 70, arrived at Netherwood sometime in 1945; he chose room number 13. It was furnished in the same way as most of the other rooms; a large wardrobe, writing table, bookshelf and single bed. Crowley soon settled into a regular daily routine. At nine each morning the housekeeper took him his breakfast, and at ten he would take a stroll in the garden. Crowley then spent most of the rest of the day sleeping in his room, where he also took his other meals. He woke as darkness fell, and sat up all night, writing letters, reading or indulging in his heroin habit. He had a permitted supply of the drug, provided by a doctor in London, with the knowledge of the police. Crowley joined Hastings Chess Club and made friends with the local grocer, who lived opposite to Netherwood, a Mr Watson, known to some as the 'Colonel', who took Crowley out for drives. He sometimes walked the short distance to the Health Hydro, Riposo, where he was befriended by the owners, the Pitcairn-Knowles. At the age of 12, the grandson of the Riposo owners, Richard, had an encounter with Crowley at Netherwood, during the birthday party of Clive, the Symonds' nephew. Richard recalls: "Clive, who was 11, invited Aleister Crowley to the party, wearing his paraphernalia; I found him of little importance, this man in fancy dress. He wore robes and beads and I thought he was a magician of some sort but he didn't do any tricks-perhaps that was just as well! The significance of the meeting did not come to me until at least 20 years later. He is often quoted now as an example of an evil man." Crowley was considered by some locals to be a person best avoided; others found him polite and apparently respectable. Mrs Symonds recalled Crowley as an easy going resident; he was not known to indulge in his beliefs and practices while in residence but ill health and old age had probably blunted his interest. Despite Crowley's controversial reputation and his custom of greeting everyone with his provocative mantra, 'Do what thou wilt shall be the whole of the law', according to Mrs Symonds, he proved to be a popular addition to the Netherwood household. However, the housekeeper, Miss Mary Richardson, a relative of the owners of Riposo, remembered him as a selfish man, who in winter used up the hot water supply at Netherwood by allowing the hot tap in his bedroom to trickle continuously, in order to warm his room.

Aleister Crowley's health deteriorated further towards the end of 1947. He developed a respiratory ailment and in spite of the ministrations of local Doctor Charnock-Smith, Crowley died on Monday, 1st December with Mrs Symonds at his side; some accounts say the mother of his son was also at his deathbed. Crowley was cremated at Brighton on the following Friday, with no religious service and only a few mourners present. A thunderstorm at Hastings greeted the mourners' return, which seemed appropriate for the passing of such a turbulent soul. Crowley had smoked a tobacco called Latakia, made with molasses and its smell lingered in his room at Netherwood for a long time after he died. When doors in the house inexplicably banged the occupants would say, 'Oh do stop it Aleister!' Netherwood was demolished in 1968 and a number of houses built on the site; the name of the Victorian house is perpetuated in the new address-Netherwood Close.

ROBERT DE MORTAIN PUB.

There is nothing available on the early history of this building at 373 The Ridge. It was formerly the Ripon Lodge Guest House, with a Ripon Garage close by. There is no date for its change of use to a pub and any personal memories of the place have been lost among its successive landlords. The pub was badly damaged in the 1987 hurricane; the licensee, Steve Thomas, who had been in possession for only three months, had just completed a £39,000 refit of the pub, carrying out the work himself. The roof was stripped of its tiles and the chimney fell through 3 floors to the basement, leaving a ruined roof and rubble in its wake and just missing a two year old boy, who was asleep in bed.

105

SANDROCK HALL

Sandrock Hall Preparatory School was built about 1875 for Baron Von Roemer. He vacated the house in 1890 and it was occupied by a Miss Dick-Lowe and Mrs Burlton; after the First World War Sandrock was used as a preparatory school for boys. It is believed that Robert Morley, who became a famous British character actor, raconteur and wit, attended the school along with a number of other prominent men. In WWII the school was commandeered as the HQ of an infantry battalion. After the war Sandrock Hall had a brief spell as a guest house during which time a scandal occurred. A mother and son had come to stay at the guest house for the purpose of committing suicide and they lay in their beds, undiscovered, for three days after the attempt. The building then became a girls' school and after this a children's home, run by a Silesian Order of Nuns. My daughter, Barbara, was an occasional visitor to Sandrock Hall in the 1960s, when she went to play with girls with whom she had made friendships at the Sacred Heart Convent, Old London Road, where she and her younger sister, Patricia and most of the boarders at Sandrock Hall went to school. Barbara's memories of Sandrock are as a fantasy place; lovely secluded gardens and plain, stark dormitories that made her think of the book, Jane Eyre. She recalls that the gates were always securely locked; whether to keep the children in or the world out she was not sure. I too had my time at Sandrock Hall; in the summer of 1965 I walked from our home on the Ridge to join Sister Elizabeth in a classroom above the former stables and take instruction in typing, so that I could help my husband with his business correspondence. Sandrock Hall is now converted into flats and large, detached modern properties stand in the once beautiful grounds.

GREAT RIDGE FARM

Great Ridge Farmhouse was built in 1658. The name Great Ridge is recorded as the residence of Reynold de Rigge in 1365. It is the nature of the life of farms that generally little happens that is of interest to the historian, other than the gradual changes that are part of social evolvement. But by chance, in 1980 Hastings Area Archeological Research Group found traces of an Elizabethan Pottery kiln in the vicinity of Great Ridge Farm. The discovery arose out of a walk taken across fields to find evidence of a Roman road, delineated by Margary in his book, Roman Ways in the Weald, as running from Westfield to Great Ridge. Evidence of the kiln was found in a field a considerable distance down Stonestile Lane; the plot was once known locally as Golden Field, due to its considerable over-growth of bracken. At the top of the field a saucer-shaped depression was found about 30 yards from the line inferred for the Roman Road. Further investigation unearthed signs of the making and firing of pottery; in July 1977 shards of pottery had been found by Farmer Ron Miles. As long ago as 1952, when excavations were being carried out to install a mains water supply to the farm at Lankhurst, the workmen said that they had dug through a ruined village. The pipe runs across the site of the kiln. The Great Ridge Farm barn is now converted into a house, the farmhouse is two dwellings and there is further, surrounding housing development, the duck farm's duck pond is now a car park. Former Hastings resident, Doris Stone, now aged 88 remembers: "My family came to live on the Ridge in 1925, when I was eight years old. Our home was 325, Great Ridge Farm, right opposite Sandrock Hall, which was a public school for boys, owned by the aunt and uncle of actor and comedian Richard Murdoch; he was often there with his stage partner Arthur Askey. My father was senior foreman for a large building firm, Homesteads Ltd and it was his job to open up the land, which is now Park Wood Road, adjacent to the stores owned by the Scollay family. I can remember this area just as fields and open land. Mr. and Mrs. Watson owned the shop on that part of The Ridge; Mr. Watson would call on his old bike for orders on a Thursday and deliver on the Friday. I can vaguely remember that it was in his stores that on occasions I would see Miss Emilie Crane, who always carried a round, wicker basket. Sometimes she'd be on the bus going to Ore Village but apart from saying "Hello"; I don't remember getting into conversation with her. I've no memory of her friends. The Ridge was a lovely place to live; always such gentle and refined people living in the district".

ST HELEN'S LODGE 369 THE RIDGE.

St Helen's Lodge, 369, the Ridge has recently been demolished to make way for a 12-apartment block. One suggestion about the origin of the house is that it was built as a residence in the latter part to the

Great Ridge Farm.

Sandrock Hall

Ore Place.

Hurst Court School for Boys.

St Margaret's Boarding School for Girls

19th century for relatives of the Spaldings, who owned nearby Ore Place. By the 1950s the house had already been adapted into flats and Mrs Eunice Hance said that she had been told that at one time the house was the home of a retired actress and that her coachman would wrap the lady in scarves and shawls, in readiness for a trot round the country lanes. The recent history of the house is rather less elegant, when it became accommodation for 'social' cases, who seriously abused the property. One day in May 2005 I was passing the house and noticed that demolition was in progress. A mound of rubbish still awaited removal; fixtures, fittings, rolls of tattered carpet, remnants of plumbing and woodwork stood beside a filthy fridge, its door open to reveal a half loaf of mouldy bread. In charge of the work I found a local man who said that he intends to develop the site. Once vacated by the subsidized tenants, the house became the victim of thieves, who removed many of the valuable Victorian, slate roof-tiles. Vandals and drug users have to be removed frequently from the ruined house by the police. The builder had hoped to be able to restore and convert the original building, adding an extension in keeping with the style of the house. However, the building was wrecked by the recent occupants; its floors urine-soaked and rotted and internal structures destroyed so the only financially viable option was to demolish and rebuild.

HURST COURT

Hurst Court School, once a school for boys, stands on the corner of The Ridge and Chowns Hill. The school was built at the behest of Doctor Read of Dover; his wife laid the foundation stone in 1863. A transcript of an advert from the Illustrated London News dated 19th September 1868 describes the school as being run by Dr Martin Reed and states: 'The school receives the sons of gentlemen from the ages of 6-18 years. First class particulars and references are available on application'. A footnote to this record mentions that Hurst Court is reputed to be haunted by the ghost of a maid who, together with her child, died of a fall from the building. Apparently only the maid is seen, not the child. French Jesuit Priests occupied Hurst Court briefly from 1883 to 1887, having been expelled from their country. According to a contemporary report the priests found Hurst Court convenient for sea bathing as it was merely one hour's walk to a convenient bay. The Jesuits moved on to new quarters at Hollington because the numbers in their community quickly outgrew the considerable accommodation at Hurst Court.

One boy who spent a brief and unhappy time at Hurst Court as a boarder was Gavin Maxwell, who in adult life wrote 'Ring of Bright Water' and many other wildlife books. Ring of Bright Water sold more than a million copies and inspired one of the best loved British films of all time. Maxwell became an instructor for the Special Operations Executive during WWII. A local resident, Mrs Eunice Hance took on the task of helping the Hurst Court matron with mending. Mrs Hance was presented with a pile of socks with holes so huge that larger supplies of grey darning wool had to be sent for from Ore Village. As she sewed, Mrs Hance noticed on the identity tags attached to the socks the names of foreign potentates and members of the Establishment. It is my loss that she cannot recall these names. Hurst Court School for Day Pupils and Boarders eventually closed in 1968 and merged with the Belmont School at Hassocks. The reason given for the closure was the poor road and rail transport system between Hastings and London. Hurst Court was re-opened as a Conference Centre in 1970. My personal association with the building began when I was working for my daughter's language school as accommodation organiser and Hurst Court was owned by a local family. They had already adapted the basement to use as a day centre for the disabled and the rest of the building was being converted to a residential school for overseas language students and other visiting groups. Hurst Court is a forbidding, grey stone edifice and its exposed position on the Ridge means high maintenance costs. When I was given a tour of the building, on a particularly cold February day in 1995, most of it was under interior renovation and refurbishment. The uppermost floors remained untouched since its days as a boarding school and the mahogany-walled, open-topped sleeping stalls for the pupils were still in situ. How stark and unwelcoming the small cubicles looked and I thought of the many new boys who must have suffered the pangs of home-sickness there, as well as terror at the thought of the phantom housemaid! The legend of the haunting persisted to the end of the 20th century, when the tale was retold to discourage the midnight, corridor wanderings of foreign students. I slept there for a few nights, to keep my daughter company when she used Hurst Court as living and teaching accommodation in July 1995. We were the first guests in the newly refurbished rooms; the beds and plump duvets were brand new and each room was equipped with a wash basin and fitted carpets; far removed from the austere arrangements for boarding school boys. Hurst Court closed as a family enterprise in September 2001 and the house, outbuildings and land were sold to a property developer for conversion to luxury flats with new houses to be built in the grounds. In January 2006, Hurst Court stands empty and deteriorating, behind ugly orange and blue hoardings. It is rumoured that a dispute about the inclusion of affordable housing in the building project is the cause of ruinous delays.

ST MARGARET'S SCHOOL

On the opposite corner to Hurst Court there is a Victorian building, which at the time of Emilie Crane's arrival on the Ridge was St Margaret's Boarding School for Girls. On early maps this building is shown as Ore House and was, for a period, the establishment of Doctor Hunt, known for his treatment of sufferers of stammering. In a publication by Longman, Green, Longman and Roberts there is a reference to the book by Hunt called, Stammering and Stuttering: Their Nature and Treatment (1865), Quoting the Doctor's prospectus for his school: "Ore House near Hastings for Juvenile Pupils. Dr Hunt has lately made arrangements to combine a superior preparatory education with his system for the treatment of defective speech and nervous affections of the voice and articulating organs in cases of children under thirteen years. These cases he receives by the year or half year. Dr Hunt continues to receive a few adult pupils for the treatment of defective speech only. Dr Hunt may be consulted in London twice every month: Further particulars on application to Ore House, Hastings." On the night of the 1861 census one of the occupants of Ore House was recorded as being Charles Dodgson, also known as Lewis Carroll, the writer of Alice in Wonderland. Following an illness at aged 17 Dodgson suffered from a stammer for the rest of his life. He had two aunts who lived at 2, Wellington Square in Hastings and he visited them frequently. The Headmistress of St Margaret's School was Miss Batty, a strict disciplinarian and according to Mrs Hance, unwilling to let her girls out to go on local visits to tea to the homes of relatives or family friends. Miss Batty kept a stern eye on the security of her girls: Mrs Hance's son was reprimanded by Miss Batty, whilst gathering sweet chestnuts one evening in the grass verge of the lane beside the school, as she believed his real intention was to spy on her girls in their dormitories. Miss Batty's school came to an end as a result of financial difficulties. After the closure of St Margaret's the building was taken over by Ledsham Court School in September 1963 but closed suddenly in 1978, due to the illness of the Headmistress, Mrs Winifred Redfearn. I had an opportunity to visit the house on an open day in May 2005; it was then a nursing home and called Hastings Cottage. One can only wonder if the person who re-named it had actually seen the house, as it bears no resemblance whatsoever to a cottage. It is an imposing Victorian mansion, set well back from the road and standing in front of a broad sweep of lawn that is bordered by a semi-circular drive. The frontage of the house is wide but on entering I found it to be a narrow building; one is no sooner in the front door than out by the back! I saw only the downstairs rooms but these are sub-divided into sitting rooms and offices, losing much of their former Victorian grace. At the rear of the house, where there was probably once a large garden there is a narrow strip of grass, bordered by a white picket fence; beyond the fence is the estate of modern houses that nowadays seems to press in on every large Victorian home. From the western aspect of 'Hastings Cottage' a view through trees shows the side windows of Hurst Court. However, the only contact between of the male and female pupils was probably at services at St Helen's Church, on the other side of the road. Local resident, Hazel Jones, remembers that during her post-war childhood she saw the girls of St Margaret's School, in uniforms of purple and gold, giggling and whispering in St Helen's pews during Sunday morning worship. Late autumn 2005 brought the news of the sudden closure of Hastings Cottage as a residence for the elderly. It seems the fate of this building to be the victim of sudden closure. It is to be re-opened as a home for the mentally ill.

ORE PLACE

Mrs Eunice Hance lives in Ore Place Farmhouse, close to the Ridge and St Helen's Church. Mrs Hance has been associated with the estate for 50 years and has great interest in its past. Ore Place Farmhouse was formerly a barn, possibly a tithe barn, bearing in mind its proximity to the church; it was later used as a coach house. Ore Place Farmhouse is approached via a drive that is headed by a yellow-brick, lodge gatehouse. The history of Ore Place goes back hundreds of years: Legend has it that a manor house, which once stood there, was owned by John of Gaunt, Duke of Lancaster in the 14th Century. In 1864 Thomas Spalding re-built Ore Place and lived there until his death in June 1887. The house and estate were then sold and was described in the agent's particulars as: "A substantial, stone-built mansion house, with exquisite pleasure grounds, in which are the remains of an ancient, ivy-clad mansion, said to have been built by John of Gaunt." Recent archeological studies have discovered that the remains are fragments of Elizabethan and Georgian structures with fanciful additions by Spalding. The property passed into the hands of a Farmer Atkinson, was later bought by the Society of Jesus in 1905/06 and subsequently occupied from 1926 by the Society of African Missions Fathers, who greatly extended the original building to meet their needs for a college.

Just a few traces of the Ore Place estate remain; a once elegant, now roofless water tower, which covered the St Helen's Spring, regarded as a Holy Well, a wall and stone archway in the gardens and a few farm outbuildings. The most significant ruins on the site are those of the original St Helen's Church, believed to have been built in the 12th or 13th century, some think its origins are 9th century. By 1869, the ancient church was suffering from damp and was inadequate for the numbers of the congregation, so a replacement was built, close to the Ridge highway. Some of the stone from the former church was incorporated in the new building, which was consecrated in 1870. For many years after its partial deconstruction, the roofless walls of the Old St Helen's Church were the scene of al fresco services in the summer and the ruins became a popular attraction to visitors. The first open air service to be held in the ruins was in August 1903, when a congregation of 300 attended; the following year this figure rose to about 1000. A curiously named Blackberry Service was held in the ruins in September 1903. In the photograph of the service at the ruins of the Old St Helen's Church in 1948, two identically dressed ladies sit in the front row. These are probably the Dawson twins, who were well known in the area. They dressed in clothes and accessories that were exactly the same, down to the smallest detail and walked about side by side so closely that there was no space between them.

115

I wonder if Emilie and her friends ever made the short walk across what was in her time a field, to see the ruined church; it was the kind of excursion I think they would have enjoyed. I visited the ruins several times in the 1970s; it appeared to me as an eerie place, surrounded by tall trees and feeling as if it was enveloped in an unearthly chill, even on the hottest summer afternoon. Many others have mentioned the phenomenon of the chill that seems to be associated with church ruins; dogs have been known to have a strong reaction against the spot. I saw the church once more in May 2005. This valuable piece of history now lies abandoned; the church tower is surrounded by metal-mesh barriers and the gate is padlocked against the further attacks of vandals. The graveyard has been excavated by badgers and the centuries-old tombstones lean amongst nettles and docks.

One of the most notable residents at Ore Place during its time as a Jesuit College was Pierre Teilhard de Chardin, paleontologist, biologist, writer, visionary and philosopher, who spent the greater part of his life trying to integrate religious experience with natural science. Long before the idea became acceptable, he saw the earth as a living entity, a notion that put him at odds with the Catholic hierarchy of his times. His paleontology interests brought de Chardin into contact with Dawson, who is famous for the Piltdown Man discovery, which later proved to be a hoax.

In May 1940 the Abbot of Ore Place and eleven of his Jesuit monks, all distressed and in tears went to the Aliens Office of Hastings Police Station. France, Belgium and Holland had fallen to the Germans and the British Isles were threatened with invasion. An anonymous police officer, who was witness to this event, recounts: "The Jesuit Monks of Ore Place were highly esteemed by the residents of the Hastings district; some of the monks, fluent in English, conducted services in the Roman Catholic Churches. Others were skilled horticulturalists and occasionally they presented the St Helen's and Royal East Sussex Hospitals with trays of vegetables. Shortly before their arrival at Hastings Police Station, the monk's abbey in France had been occupied by the German Army. Under the provisions of the Aliens Registration Act, all aliens were required to leave the South East Defence Area forthwith. In compliance with the regulation the abbot

and the monks wished to register their change of address to a monastery in the Midlands. The amendments of the monks' registration certificates took some time. After the conclusion of the clerical work involved, the abbot made a fond farewell to Hastings Police as he solemnly blessed all those present and drove off in a van."
Ore Place remained unoccupied until it was commandeered in wartime by the Royal Army Service Corp as their regimental HQ and record office. About 130 civilians were appointed as clerks in these offices; all of them being required to swear an oath as prescribed by the Official Secrets Act and the Defence Regulations. However, as the anonymous contributor remembers, not all took this oath seriously: "In mid-June 1943 an inquiry was conducted into a male civilian employee in the RASC Records Office, who was suspected of bribery and corruption and breaches of several Defence Regulations. This enquiry was dealt with by several CID officers serving in the Hastings Borough Police Force. The local father of a RASC soldier had reported to the Detective Inspector that he had been approached by a male civilian, employed in the RASC postings department. For a substantial sum this man offered to arrange for the father's son to be permanently posted in the UK for the duration of the war. The complainant declined and was disgusted with this offer, also suspecting that the RASC employee had made more such unfair and disloyal transactions with local parents of soldiers serving in the regiment. Investigations were made into the serious allegations. The detective officers conducted a search of the RASC postings records for details of any of the regiment's personnel, whose parents lived locally and who had been posted to units in the UK. The parents were then interrogated and it was established that some of them had bribed the employee for a favourable posting for their son or other relative. The civilian RASC employee was arrested and charged with numerous serious offences and committed for trial at Sussex Assizes. He was refused bail and a heavy sentence was imposed on the offender. This prosecution was restricted to a 'secret' level because the location of the RASC Regimental HQ and its record office had to be safeguarded at all costs and public morale had to be maintained, so there was never any report in the local press about this unusual case". This sounds very like the plot of an early episode of the ITV television programme, Foyle's War, the police detective series set in WWII Hastings. Certainly, this factual case was not an isolated incidence of the kind of offence but it

demonstrates the authenticity of the series. As I write, the nation is still in shock at the reports of armed police officers shooting dead a terrorist suspect on a train. Yet, in living memory this was a possibility that existed on the Home Front every day, as the following anonymous account shows: "One morning in 1942 I was on duty in Hastings Police Station. A Royal Canadian Military Police Sergeant came in with a private in handcuffs. The sergeant requested that his prisoner, who was facing charges of desertion, missing a draft, insubordination and loss of army equipment, should be confined in a police cell until he could be handed over to an armed escort from the Ore Place RASC HQ on the Ridge, to face a court martial there. The prisoner complained to me that during the train journey from London the sergeant had sat aiming a loaded pistol at him the whole time. The sergeant explained that during the train journey from the Midlands to London the prisoner had tried to escape several times by attempting to open the compartment windows. The sergeant had strongly warned his prisoner not to do this again but he had remained very defiant and restless. The train was due to stop at every station en route and once more the prisoner had attempted to open the carriage window. To put a stop to this behaviour the sergeant had loaded his .38 service revolver and warning his prisoner he would be shot if he tried to escape again, he held him at pistol point until the train arrived at Hastings Station. I never heard what sentence the Court Martial at Ore Place passed on the prisoner".

The army authorities finally vacated Ore Place in 1986, it was demolished in 1987 and the October storm of that year further devastated the estate and brought down hundreds of mature trees that had contributed to the beauty of the Ridge. Planning permission to develop the Ore Place site was granted and when road-building work was underway it was Mrs Eunice Hance who drew the attention of the local authorities to the connection between the famous French priest and the location. Due to her intervention, one of the roads in the new estate is named De Chardin Drive. The new housing estate is called Abbey Heights. One saving grace in the loss of Ore Place is that a small, derelict farm and its remarkable outbuildings, once part of the estate, was preserved and is now a thriving horticultural training centre, called Friary Gardeners, for people with learning difficulties.

ST HELEN'S CHURCH.

The new St Helen's Church was erected in 1869, with a tall spire, which became a prominent landmark in the district. The church, designed by local architects Habershon and Brock, was built of local bluestone with bath-stone dressings. Preserved in the new building is a relic from the former St Helen's Church. It is a monumental brass, to be seen on the north wall of the sanctuary, depicting the portraits of a man and woman in prayer. The brass is believed to be the second oldest of its kind in Sussex. Just beyond the church and at the rear of Ore Place gatehouse a corrugated building was erected in 1871 to be used as a school, it was probably constructed to the same pattern as St Peter's Church at Baldslow; the tin school has now vanished. In 1888 the children moved to a school house that stands beside the St Helen's Church, the building is now the church hall and used for various social meetings and a playgroup, brownies and a youth club. In the sixties the St Helen's Church spire was in need of costly repairs. The funds were not available to carry out the restoration work and the requisite regular inspections of the structure so the spire was removed in 1967. It was replaced by the Sussex cap seen today. Parishioner Mrs Winnie West had the weather-cock re-gilded and replaced on the new roof cap. St Helen's Church marked its centenary in September 1970 with a period of celebratory events that ranged from consecration and thanksgiving services to a sports day with barbeque and a centenary dinner at Beauport Park Hotel, on the Ridge. The present rector of St Helen's Church, Chris Key, said that the life of the church today is vibrant and follows a modern form of worship.

HASTINGS CEMETERY

Hastings Cemetery was opened on 28th November 1856 and it was agreed with local churches that henceforth burials in churchyards should cease. Originally the cemetery had two separate chapels, one for Church of England members, and the other for Dissenters. The two chapels, the two cemetery lodges and the boundary walls were all built from local sandstone, reputedly from Hastings cliffs, when alterations were being carried out at the seafront. The first person buried in the cemetery was stonemason John Smith, on 2nd December 1856. He was reported to have supplied some of the stone for the building of the cemetery's boundary wall from a quarry at Fairlight. The original area enclosed for burial ground was 19 acres and in 1884 a further 9 acres were added. In 1890 the addition of further ground brought the cemetery area up to seventy two and a half acres, 11 of which remained undeveloped. In 1906 the superintendent's house and office were altered to provide additional office and mess rooms and a separate house was built for the superintendent. A further four and a half acres were taken in on the 8th May 1940, as a potential war graves cemetery.

A crematorium for the Hastings Cemetery had been considered as early as 1902 but no action was taken. The matter was raised again in 1925 and yet again in 1938, with a view to building on the adjacent Ore Villa Farm. A design for the crematorium by architect Holland W Hobbs was accepted and an application for a loan of £12,150 from the government was made in May 1939 but it was disallowed in January 1940; with the nation at war there were more pressing considerations. The big freeze in the winter of 1947 that coated everything with heavy layers of frozen rain brought down many trees in the cemetery, one falling tree killed local man, Jim Evans.

In 1948 ground that had belonged to Adam's Fruit Farm was purchased by Hastings Borough Council for inclusion in the cemetery. A post war plan suggested for a small cost it would be possible to convert the two existing chapels to include a crematorium. The new building was to comprise a committal room, crematory, clergy vestries, funeral director's staff room and new public toilets. Although the stone used to build the chapels had been exposed to 100 years of the harsh weather conditions of the Ridge it was still in excellent condition and the new stone and Gothic style of the extension matched the original building perfectly. The crematorium was declared open by the Earl of Verulam on 5th November 1955. Records show that the total interments up until March 1957 were 66,361. The crematorium began to have an effect on the demand for burial plots and in 1975, following the demolition of Thorpe's plant nursery, which stood just outside the western border of the cemetery, the vacant site was developed into a formal garden of remembrance for cremated remains. Four years later a local controversy arose when Hastings Borough Council undertook a 'tidying up scheme', part of which was the removal of some of the oldest or deteriorating headstones. The monument to Whistler's mother, who died in Hastings, was placed elsewhere in the cemetery. Also under threat were the gravestones of Harry Furniss, the cartoonist and caricaturist who had created illustrations for the works of Lewis Carroll and Punch Magazine, Canon Bullock, the Church in the Wood expert, James Rock, the coach builder of White Rock and members of the local, beneficent Blackman family.

My first visit to the cemetery was in February 1956, to attend a family funeral. It was a severe winter and the ground was snow covered, with the bitter wind blowing that was so much part of Ridge winters, when our climate was colder. In spite of this, I was struck by the beauty of the cemetery, with its plantations of huge trees, including, at the highest point, a long avenue of pines and a view over vast tracts of countryside, to the Sussex Weald and Rye Bay. I used to live about 10 minute's walk from the cemetery and in the spring and summer of 1956 I substituted the lack of a nearby public park by taking my baby in her pram round the broad paths of the cemetery. In those days wild flowers; primroses, violets, anemones, bluebells and foxgloves abounded under the trees and in uncultivated patches of soil, reminders of the ground's woodland history. The cemetery has moved with the times and in 1995 it began to provide environmentally friendly funerals, in one acre of land, set aside for woodland burials, using biodegradable coffins and shrubs for headstones and the growth of woodland plants and flowers is encouraged.

BURSLEM MONUMENTAL STONEMASONS

Thomas Burslem was born in 1826 to William Burslem, Master stonemason of Staffs. Thomas arrived in Kent, allegedly on foot, in about 1845, to work on the sandstone buildings being erected in the area. He later acquired his own yard and in 1880 his son Albert (A Burslem) founded The Company as a monumental mason at 77, Calverly Road, Tunbridge Wells. The new company continued to work on the many sandstone buildings in Tunbridge Wells and the surrounding villages and small towns. Albert suffered from poor health and in 1898 his 18 year-old son Robert took over. By dint of hard work Robert seems to have turned around the fortunes of the business but as a result of the Great War it went into a decline and the workforce was

St Helen's Church, prior to
the removal of the steeple.

Open air service at St Helen's Church ruins, 1949.

St Helen's Church former schoolroom.

The gatehouse of Ore Place.

Wartime wedding at St Helen's Church.

Cemetery trees bent and broken by ice. 1947.

Postcard view of Hastings Cemetery. c.1906.

Burslem Monumental Masons.

St Helen's Post Office and the Hastings High School for Girls.

reduced to 8 elderly men. Robert went into the army and the memorial department of the business was run by his wife, assisted by a man in the technical department, until her husband was demobilised and returned to rebuild trade, no doubt aided by the huge demand for post-war monumental masonry. The Imperial War Graves Commission was set up almost immediately after the end of the Great War to deal with the enormous quantity of remains of men from all over the British Empire, who had been killed in the trenches in Flanders and on many other battlefields. Land was purchased for cemeteries and the dead were exhumed from their temporary resting places and re-interred in these war cemeteries. A small headstone of Portland stone was erected over each grave, engraved with the regimental badge, and the name and number of each man. If the relatives wished, a religious emblem of the deceased's faith and two lines of a personal inscription could be added. Burslem still hold the original templates of the regimental badges that the stonemasons used for the war graves' headstones. Between 1921 to 1927 these headstones were loaded onto lorries for dispatch to Dover at the rate of 500 per week; a statistic which brings home the magnitude of the loss of life in World War One. Burslem also built some of the major war memorials throughout Northern France, at the Somme and Gallipoli and they worked all the stone and the 160 name panels for the Menin Gate at Ypres in Belgium, completed in 1927. The gates were designed by Sir Reginald Blomfield, who at one time lived at Rye. The list of overseas cemeteries for which Burslem provided many thousands of headstones is an historic roll-call of the sites of famous battles. Among them are Etaples, Flanders, Vignancourt, Delville Wood, Messines Ridge, Dar-Es-Salem, Algiers, and Beiruit. Included in this list are commissions for stonemasonry for WWI War Memorials for a number of British towns and villages. In the mid-1920s Burslem acquired a number of other masonry companies in the area amongst them Monk's and also, opposite, Bennett's at 232 the Ridge, which had been operating in Hastings since the 1880s, making it one of the oldest companies still trading in Hastings. In the 1970s Monk's building was demolished and the business was amalgamated with the showrooms and workshops across the road. The former Monk's site is now the location of Geewoods Surfacing. By 1929, due to the onset of the depression, the large commissions that Burslem received from great houses and prestigious rural and London Buildings began to decline. Robert Burslem did his best to maintain his employees by providing extensive work on his own property and by hiring his men out to other companies but the work force was reduced from 60 in 1934 to 30 by 1938. The onset of WWII caused a further reduction in work, which was mostly confined to monumental and building repairs. The labour force in the business was reduced to 15 men. After the war there was a back-log of memorial work: As well as personal memorials in churchyards and cemeteries, additional panels were required for names on public war memorials all over the area. Burslem also supplied worked stone for the repair of churches, chapels, banks and hotels, private and stately homes, municipal buildings and schools. In the post war years the taste in grave memorials began to change to un-carved headstones or crosses with brief inscriptions; the use of marble for headstones in church yards was banned in 1968. Branches of Burslem began to close and Robert died at the age of 80 in 1960, leaving the business to his widow. It was later decided that offices and workshops should be concentrated at Tunbridge Wells and Hastings. It seems Burslem has continued to move with the times: In 1994 they employed Kay Wright, one of the few female letter carvers in the stonemasonry trade. Since 2000 Burslem's fortunes have improved, with the work force back up to 30 operatives including the occasional apprentice. The business has experienced an influx of orders for new building, restoration work as well as running a thriving granite and marble masoning department, bringing in work from many different sources. Burslem continue to provide the highest standard of home-worked, carved and lettered memorials to this day. A young, professional and qualified team has evolved, taking Burslem and stonemasonry on into the 21st century.

ST HELEN'S MEMORIES

Christine Winter- nee Redhead- grew up at 219, Homefield Terrace, The Ridge, with her sister Joan, Tim Tidmarsh's mother. Their house was next door to Allen's General Store and Post Office, run by their uncle, Jack Allen; the store still exists but is no longer a Post Office. Christine's memories are of a time when the Ridge seemed like a country village and she recalled playing with the gardener's children at Ore Place. For a number of years Joan Tidmarsh organised the Ridge May Queen Pageant; Christine said that her sister started in this kind of venture very early by presenting plays in the woods, near to the St

Helen's church ruins. 'There were two tall trees that supported a curtain to conceal the stage and people came to see us perform. I was Sleeping Beauty once and I always remember someone in the audience saying of me, 'She moved her foot and she's supposed to be dead.' We also did nativity plays'. Joan organised the Christmas carol singing group that went from house to house, to raise money for what was then called The Waifs and Strays, now known as The Children's Society. Christine said that all the big houses had servants and that at the top of Parkwood Road there were charcoal burners and she and Joan used to take a large, old pram, so that they could collect the wood chippings the men left. Christine mentioned walking from the Ridge to the Ore Village end of Victoria Avenue, where a man called Mr Cork used to iron her father's stiffly-starched, detachable collars for his shirts.

The Shaftsbury Home for Ragged Boys (now Osbourne House) on the corner of the Ridge and Elphinstone Road always had a marvellous firework display on November 5th and everybody went to see it. During the war there was an underground air raid shelter in the garden of the home and after the boys were evacuated Ridge locals used the shelters to sleep in at night. At the outbreak of WWII Christine and Joan were working at Boots, the chemist in London Road, St Leonards; Christine in the library section and Joan in the dispensary. Joan remained in her job as it was one of national importance but Christine joined the land army and went by train to a farm at Doleham, returning each night, as her mother did not want her to sleep away from home. Later in the war, the local Home Guard, which was in the charge of Major Hocking, a Great War veteran, had a Head Quarters at the parish rooms, adjacent to St Helen's Church. The Canadian regiment, stationed nearby, was the Royal Hamilton Light Infantry and there was also the British regiment, the Royal Lancashires, who were billeted at Sandrock Hall. Christine said, 'Our local Home Guard had an attachment to the Canadian soldiers, who, I think, were billeted at Hydneye House and they and the British soldiers used to go on manoevres together. My mum was very good to the boys from overseas and on many an evening she fed them and they played crib with my dad. Being so far from home they loved it. We met some lovely Canadian boys; many went from Hastings on the Dieppe raid in August 1942 and didn't return. Beastly war!'

Christine said that both she and Joan joined the Women's Voluntary Service and collected supplies from the WVS kitchen in St Leonards, to run a canteen for the Home Guard in St Helen's Church room. Later in the war they opened the canteen seven nights a week, between 11.00pm and 1.00am, so they tried to get a few hour's sleep in the early evenings, to prepare for the late nights. Christine said, 'We thoroughly enjoyed the work and the army would see us home safely afterwards. Joan was married in 1943 to Tom Tidmarsh, who was in the RAF. We were on tenterhooks the night before, until he arrived home; you never knew if leave would be cancelled. The Home Guard formed a guard of honour as the bride and groom left the church, I was a bridesmaid and my mum made a wonderful wedding breakfast and cake, especially wonderful considering the problems with rationing. But life wasn't all fun and games; there were the tip and run raiders and I remember one night the church bells at Westfield were rung by mistake and everyone thought that the Germans had arrived, as this was the wartime warning to the nation, should an invasion occur.'

THE GIRLS' HIGH SCHOOL AND THE CLEEVE

A very prominent building on the Ridge, opposite to the cemetery, was a red-brick, Victorian school, built in 1901, later becoming Hastings High School for Girls. (A comprehensive book on the history of the High School and its successor, Helenswood, is available for purchase, directly from the school librarian.) The High School's architectural style was somewhat forbidding and it remained erroneously in the memory of Judith Rance, who stayed briefly in the Cleeve as a child after the war, as being the town's lunatic asylum! By the 1930s the school's intake had outgrown the building and extensions were added. Post WWII, yet further classrooms were needed and in 1945 Hastings Council bought from owner, Mrs R M Malony, the Victorian house, the Cleeve and five acres of land that were adjacent to the High School. Local historian, Brian Lawes gives a detailed description of the Cleeve: 'It was an imposing stucco house with a low-pitched slate roof, its principal rooms were on two floors; there were also attics and cellars. On the north side of the house facing the Ridge there was a porch with square Corinthian columns, which opened onto a carriage drive. Inside on the left was a study facing east and the drawing room with windows facing east and south. On the right were a cloakroom and a beautiful curving staircase with wrought iron banisters and a polished wood rail. Overlooking the gardens on the south side was a magnificent room with French windows that opened onto a gravel terrace that was under a veranda framed with roses. Below this was the lawn, pool and a rockery. Through a stand of trees a lovely view of the Fire Hills and the sea as far as Beachy Head was visible. Beyond a baize door on the west side of the house was the kitchen with a blue and white tiled range and huge floor to ceiling cupboards. There was also a scullery, dairy and leading from the kitchen, a steep staircase to the servants' attic quarters. Everywhere was fine Victorian plaster decoration; ceiling roses and friezes, marble fireplaces and brass fittings to the doors. There were Greek and Roman style friezes illustrating ancient history'.

ST HELEN'S RECTORY, NOW HELENSWOOD NURSING HOME.

This solid stone edifice formerly known as Lorne Villa was the home of the St Helen's Church rector from about 1892 to 1980. At 195 The Ridge it stands close to the former site of the Cleeve. Joan Head, nee Hills, grew up under the care of a foster mother at 217 the Ridge before the war. She remembers, when a child, helping to make cakes for tea parties that were held on the St Helen's Rectory lawn, for the Women's Institute or the Mothers' Union. The Rector, the Rev. Graham was well known for his generous help to the poorer members of his parish. Joan Head cleaned the rectory in later years when Rev. Spray was the rector; she remembers the interior of the house as being in a grand Victorian style with about six bedrooms. The rectory was considered too large for its purpose and was sold in about 1980 and converted to a nursing home for 16 residents. The present rectory is at 226 Elphinstone Road. Mrs Wilson, a former churchwarden at St Helen's Church became a resident of Helenswood Nursing Home and recently died there, aged 108.

LENNOX HOUSE 141, THE RIDGE.

The few Victorian houses remaining on the Ridge are almost all converted into flats or used as institutions, with the exception of Lennox House, built in 1865, on the corner of Pine Avenue and the

The Cleeve.

Lennox House.

Coghurst Gatehouse. c.1915

Fairlight Sanatorium.

Ridge. At one point in its history Lennox House was the home of W. Vincent Edward the Chief Engineer and General Manager of Hastings Tramways. It has been said that the house had its own tram-bay, from which the manager departed for his office in the town. Reliable sources say the truth of the anecdote about the private tram bay is suspect but I include it for further debate; of such is local history made! The external woodwork and shutters of Lennox House were treated with heavy duty tram paint at one point, which proved very difficult to remove when the house was restored. The beams in the basement of the house are stamped HTC, for Hastings Tramways Company. From 1943 Mrs Margaret King, grandmother to Mrs Enid Eldridge of Beaulieu Farm, lived in Lennox House, after she was bombed out of her house in Silverhill. She had been widowed some time previously and left with nine children, the youngest only three years old. Before moving to the Ridge she had run a small, private school at Silverhill. Her late husband was the principal of the School of Science at Hastings Fishmarket. He was pictured in a brochure of the time as being the last person to ride a penny-farthing bicycle in public in Hastings. Mrs King moved to Brede in 1952.

COGHURST GATE HOUSE.

The demolition of Coghurst Hall, two miles off the Ridge commenced in the early 1950s. The Hall's gatehouse remained in place, opposite to the Ridge entrance to Victoria Avenue until the late 1950s. The Moon family was the last to occupy one half of the gatehouse, which was built to accommodate two families. 'Very cramped living space' a local remembers. This impressive structure disappeared to make way for the entrance to a new East Kent bus garage. An off license, previously a car showroom, now occupies the spot where the gatehouse stood. The former bus garage became Dickie's Discount Supermarket for a brief period. The grand opening of the store in the early 1970s was the occasion of the biggest jamboree this spot could ever have witnessed; after touring Ore Village, an open-topped, double-decker bus stood in the supermarket car park, with a five-piece, Womble's jazz band playing on the top deck. Crowds arrived to watch the Dagenham Girl Pipers, who marched and skirled outside the store. This opening set the hectic tone for the supermarket and its closure came as a relief to neighbouring residents. The building became and remains a wholesale and retail timber store.

NEWTON ST LOE. 63 THE RIDGE

From 1962 to 1982 I lived at 63, The Ridge, a red-brick, late-Victorian house on the corner of Victoria Avenue. Many years before, the house, once named Newton St Loe, had been occupied by Mr Green, who owned a butcher's shop in Ore Village. Immediately before my family and I took up residence, number 63 had been occupied by Mr Marriot, a builder and decorator. The upper exterior of the house is now pebble-dashed as the hurricane of 1987 stripped the western side of the house of its period, terracotta hung tiles, which always chattered madly in high winds, and threw them across the main road like missiles. At the end of the garden there is a long workshop, now enlarged, which had been built as a stable, from where horses and carts were once hired out. When the present owner of the workshop, motor engineer Mr Derek Burt excavated its floor he discovered a large storage tank that had supplied petrol to a pump, which used to stand outside the stable door.

KENT HATCH. 21 THE RIDGE

From 1955 we lived at 21 The Ridge, in a ground floor maisonette, part of a converted, mid-Victorian house that still bears its original name of Kent Hatch. Before we took the tenancy the flat had been occupied by a Mr Morley, who died in the ground-floor, front bedroom. A neighbour regaled me with such lurid details of his prolonged and vociferous departure from this world that I was left with a permanent dread of the room. The property's large rooms, high ceilings with intricate mouldings, wealth of interior woodwork and big marble fireplaces made re-decorating, furbishing and furnishing a discouraging prospect for a hard up young couple with a new baby. From the description of the Cleeve it seems that Kent Hatch was a more modest version of the same style of architecture, lacking the grand entrance and the beautiful grounds. At some time in its history, certainly by 1934, Kent Hatch was converted into two self-contained flats and a semi-detached house. At this time number 21 was occupied by Mr Grist and the flat above, 21a, by William Fraser Strickland. The semi-detached residence, number 19, was home for many years, including during our neighbouring occupancy, to Detective Inspector Stanley Copper of the Hastings Borough Police. He was one of the old style police officers and I was very nervous of his authoritarian manner. Even more so when my kitten dug holes in the rows of seeds that Mr Copper, a keen gardener, had just sown. Our ground-floor flat included access to the house cellar, wherein we found a sentimental, Victorian painting called The Elopement that I still treasure today.

ORATAVA HOUSE THE RIDGE

Opposite to Kent Hatch was a piece of rough ground nicknamed 'Arvy-Tarvy' by the local children. I discovered that a large property called Oratava House had stood there. In the 1950s we used to walk our dog across the vacant plot and sections of the coloured, mosaic-tiled front path and the remains of cellars were still visible. Oratava House can clearly be seen on the aerial photograph taken in 1927 but it has been impossible to find out the reason for its disappearance; whether it was the result of bombing or demolition there is no clue. It was certainly gone by the mid-1940s; life-long Ore resident, Angie Quinnell remembers playing among the foundations of the house during that period and local lads, racing under the name of the Ridge Eagles, had a cycle track there for a while. Sandown School now occupies the site of Oratava House.

METHODIST CHURCH.

St Helen's Methodist Church stands in a particularly exposed spot on the corner of the Ridge and Clifton Road. The new Methodist Church was companion to one that already stood at Old Top Road, a place marked on contemporary maps as Fairlight Down, the former name of Ore Village. The foundation stone for the new church was laid in June 1886 by Mr Henry Beck, the father of Hastings Methodism and the first services were held in the following early November. In spite of the building's noble appearance it had been constructed with economy in mind, a measure which proved to be unwise, as the strong winds that sweep off the sea and up Ore Valley took their toll of the structure. The legacy of this false economy continues today. The name of the church was changed to St Helen's Wesleyan Chapel in 1913. Due to mass evacuation of the population of the town in WWII, St Helen's Methodist Church, as it was called by then, was closed during the war. The pews were removed and it served as a youth club until the friends of St Helen's came together and decided to try and open the church again. The lower school room was opened for use as a church in October 1948. Meanwhile, a full renovation was taking place in the church above. The congregation was full to overflowing when the church proper was opened in January 1951. Over the past century and a half renovations, extensions and improvements have been made to the building and today the church has an active following and provides many secular services to the community.

THE WHITE MILL, ORE.

One of the trustees of the St Helen's Wesleyan Chapel was miller John Wesley Thomas, who worked at the White Mill that once stood on the other side of the road from the new church. As well as serving on the trust, Thomas provided funds towards the building of the new church. The mill was burnt down on 16th May 1900, and the event was described in dramatic detail by a reporter on the local newspaper. 'When I first arrived on the scene dense clouds of smoke and a little flame were issuing from out of the top of the structure but gradually the dark red fire showed itself. The glass was shattered in the little windows and then the draught was increased. The roar of the fire grew louder and louder and the heat became more and more unbearable, steadily driving the crowd backwards.' And what a crowd it must have been. Although this part of the Ridge is not its highest point, the smoke must have been visible from miles around and locals surely turned out in droves to see such an exciting spectacle. The reporter went on: 'The doors soon opened and then the scene was a splendid one, the interior of the mill could be seen to be a veritable furnace, nothing but a mass of flame was visible. Here and there a tiny jet of flame or small curling wreaths of smoke crept from between the woodwork; the wind was fanning the fire, so that in very minutes the gallery and other parts were seen to be well ablaze. The flames crept up and caught the sails and then the end approached. The whole was almost completely enveloped in a wild mantle of fire. The heat thrown out was tremendous and at times the black smoke clouds were overpowering. Then, crash! Down came the whole concern. It did not sway at all but gave one the impression of a huge concertina being compressed. At the moment of the fall a heat wave of fearful power was caused and everyone was compelled to retire in haste, covering his face. The adjoining buildings, which had also been steadily burning and were

Aerial view of the eastern end of the Ridge. c.1927

St Helen's Methodist Church at Ore.

Ore White Mill,
destroyed by fire in 1901.

Holman's confectionery workshop, Ore Village. c.1930

James Kemp, butcher. Ore Village. c.1925

Vi Pratt, Ore Village Land Army Girl.

Leslie and George Potter, Church Street boys in wartime.

well tarred, collapsed. The lower part of the mill, of brick, was simply a seething furnace, the machinery being white hot. Rats and mice crawled about and ran hither and thither in their fright.' The brick base of the mill survived and a dwelling called Mill House stands now on the site, next to Sandown School. John Wesley Thomas became ill with millers' lung, retired from his trade and established a business as a photographer in George Street. Hastings.

BOOT REPAIR SHOP.

Next to the White House, the last house on the northern side of the Ridge is a small, detached brick building; currently a hairdresser's called the Hair Shed. And indeed it is not much more than a shed. In the mid-1930s it was occupied by Mr Medhurst, who ran a boot repair shop from the premises. It was probably he who was still working there when I moved to the Ridge in 1955. He was very elderly, wore a leather apron and used tools and equipment that looked as if they came from the previous century, including a heavy treadle sewing machine. When the cobbler retired the premises was briefly an antiques shop and for a long period, a clock and watch repair workshop, run by Robert Wren of Victoria Avenue. In the 1930s this eastern end of the Ridge was seen as very 'trade' and working class and, to a much less extent, the impression persists today.

FAIRLIGHT SANATORIUM, NOW BARRINGTON HOUSE REST HOME.

Set back from the road by the Red Lake traffic lights is a detached Victorian house, built in 1896, on what was then called Fairlight Down. The house was originally named the Hall and confusion sometimes arose between this property and Fairlight Hall, built in the valley between Pett and Fairlight. In 1905 the house was converted into the Fairlight Hall Convalescent Home and later it became a sanatorium, with 22 beds for tuberculosis patients. The ground across the road was used as gardens for the patients to work in. The apartment buildings, South View Court, now stand on this spot, where an iron-reddened stream of water used to pool, giving the area its name. In the early 1950s Fairlight Sanatorium was still used for the long term treatment of TB patients and when passing by it was possible to see some of them sleeping outside in all weathers, on the verandas of small huts, mounted on turntables. During WWII the sanatorium was used as a convalescent home for military patients. In the late fifties the sanatorium closed and its patients' recreation room became Ore Village Public Library. In 1979 a road widening scheme took away most of the southern section of the house grounds and the DIY store, B&Q, stands in what was formerly gardens on its northern side and the house became a rest home.

ORE VILLAGE

Ore Village once had a wide variety of shops, services and professions that would have met nearly all of the needs of the Lavender Cottage household. It was just a short trolley bus ride from the cottage to Ore, to find several butchers, greengrocers and grocers, a fishmonger, a boot and shoe shop, ironmongers, seed and corn merchant, drapers, a post office, newsagent, bakers and confectioners, a watchmaker and a chemist. There were two banks, a doctor, solicitor and a lending library.

Peter Paine, who was born in 1933, has lived in Ore Village almost all of his life. His grandfather was Jimmy Kemp, a slaughter man, butcher, Hastings Town Councillor and local sportsman. Mr Kemp ran the butcher's shop that was, until recently, Gray's Butchers at 482, Old London Road. (Currently it is an all-day-breakfast 'caff'.) During the late 1930s - early 1940s, Mr Kemp used the brick-built base of the burned-out White Mill on the Ridge as a slaughter house and the field behind it was known as Kemp's Field. Peter Paine remembers that his grandfather was a blunt-spoken man but also very kind; he was known to send, discreetly, the gift of a parcel of meat to families who were in difficult straits. During the war Peter and his mother lived with her parents, in the accommodation above the butcher's shop; Peter remembers running into Holman's, the tobacco and confectionery wholesaler in the Ore shopping parade, to shelter from German planes that were machine-gunning through the village. While living at the butcher's shop Peter escaped death or serious injury on two further occasions. The first time was when a bomb was dropped on a house on the corner of Canute Road and Fairlight Avenue. Peter cannot remember the exact date but it might have well been May 3rd 1942, when Ore suffered a heavy bombing raid. Blast shattered the window above Peter's bed and the shards of glass ripped the bedding to shreds; it was his good fortune that a bad cold had caused him to sleep in his mother's room that night. The date of Peter's next lucky escape was Wednesday July 19th 1944: At 1.17pm he was standing in front of the large window at the back of his grandfather's butcher's shop when he saw a Spitfire in pursuit of a flying bomb, trying to bring it down. Peter saw the flying bomb become suddenly enveloped in a massive cloud of black gas and golden flame, with a simultaneous, shattering explosion but miraculously the glass in the window where he was standing did not break. Parts of the flying bomb fell on Godden's Farm, now the Broomgrove Housing Estate and on Pine Avenue, causing one serious casualty and six cases of minor injury. Miss Commin, the Headmistress of the Girls' High School was outside during the event and escaped injury by sheltering in a ditch. The spitfire's pursuit and 'kill' over Ore is featured in a 14-minute, contemporary film that also shows other wartime exploits that occurred over the town. In the film, which can be purchased from the Imperial War Museum, familiar landmarks of Hastings and St Leonards are clearly visible. Jimmy Kemp gave up the butcher's shop sometime between 1945 and 1948. (I wonder if he is the butcher mentioned in some of Emilie Crane's letters.) Peter has very warm memories of the Ore Village trading community of his childhood. He recalls it as a friendly place, where people had respect for each other, regardless of social or financial standing.

Daisy Jarman lived from early infancy and for the start of her married life in Greville Road in Ore Village. She attended the infants' school in the village and later went to the Central School in Priory Road. In 1929 Daisy took a job at J Holman and Son, the manufacturing and wholesale confectioner, whose premises were at 464 Old London Road, in the Ore Village trading community. The boiling room where the sweets were made was at the back of the shop; Daisy contributed to this book the rare image of the workshop from her family photograph collection. It was at Holman that she met her husband Richard, who can be seen in the background of the photograph; co-worker Fred Heselden is in the foreground. Holman's boiled sweets were famous in the locality; humbugs, pear drops, acid drops and the made to their own recipe, 'chest relievers.' Daisy eventually became the manageress of the shop, which also sold other brands of confectionery, tobacco and groceries. Due to the shortage of sugar in WWII Holman's manufacture of sweets came to an end but was resumed after the war. Daisy said that at one point in the war the fields around Rock Lane, then just an unmade track, were used as a tented camp site for hundreds of soldiers, probably prior to the D-Day landings. She said, 'One morning I saw a young soldier emerge from a tent, you could see he had just washed and shaved and he was singing in a most beautiful voice, I wish I could remember the song - something about blue skies and the clouds rolling away. One day, suddenly all the soldiers disappeared and I wondered how many returned safely from the invasion and if the young singer was among them.' (Could any of these 1944 soldiers have been aware that when Napoleon threatened our shores, these same fields were an encampment for anti-invasion troops in 1779?) Daisy left Holman's in 1959; in the early 1960s she joined the Royal Air Force, as part of the living-out clerical staff. Holman and Son closed and became a launderette and later a second hand furniture shop. It is now the hardware section of Nice Price. Daisy has vivid memories of her 30 years of working in Ore Village: 'The less sick of the Fairlight Sanatorium tuberculosis patients were sometimes allowed out to shop and they would come to the sweet shop at Christmas, to buy gifts. Some patients carried with them the sputum cups into which they had to spit after coughing. Attitudes to such things were different then'. Daisy spoke about Mr Turk, the Ore grocer, who sold broken biscuits from a huge barrel outside his shop: She heard customers advising each other against buying the biscuits, as passing dogs used the barrel as a convenience! Mrs Noakes, a tall untidy woman, who ran the little general store in Church Street in the valley below Ore Village, bought her confectionery stocks from Holman; she would buy only small quantities and never on credit, as she was proud that she, 'never owed nobody a penny.' Daisy said, on seeing the photograph of Emilie Crane that her face was familiar and it's possible that Emilie, a smoker, was a customer at Holman and Son.

In spite of some advances in social conditions by the 1920s, many of Ore's residents still lived in relative poverty. In the Local History Group publication, Hastings Voices, Alf Hodd, who was born in Ore Village in 1922, gave an account of home life and his parents' and neighbours' struggles to make ends meet. 'Almost everybody had an allotment and many householders reared pigs; children would go from house to house collecting swill for the pigs, for which they received a penny from the pig owners and a free joint of pork at Christmas. During the depression many men were out of work and the Means Test Officer would call on the household to check the family had nothing of value they could sell before they were granted any aid. Many men took to illegally catching rabbits as a source of family food, to raise a small household income or money for beer. A whole culture of language, habits and the ownership of ferrets and cunning, mongrel hunting dogs was based on this pursuit. Appearances at the magistrates' courts for stealing rabbits were common but the fines imposed were rarely paid. Many families lived on 'tick' (credit) and a poor diet, lack of adequate clothing and home heating was common. Clothing and footwear was passed down from one child to another with no regard to its fit, condition or gender suitability. Ridicule from other children was rare; each looked as scruffy as the other. Alf Hodd remembers going with his grandmother to the Central Police station to get a pair of boots from the Police Fund as he called it, believing at the time that it was the policemen who provided the boots out of their own money. He recalled that the Police Sergeant used to say to the grandmother, after handing over the boots, "Now take him up to St Helen's Police Station, (this used to be on the Winchelsea Road junction of the Ridge) and get his toy". At St Helen's Police Station they had books and trains and the policeman used to give you a toy'.

Hastings Municipal Hospital, later called St Helen's Hospital was situated on Frederick Road, in the valley below Ore Village. The original building, opened in 1837, had begun its life as the Union Workhouse and an overnight shelter to tramps. Ore people, who were children during the depression, have clear memories of the brief presence in the community of men and sometimes women, who eked out a shabby existence by constantly wandering from one area workhouse to the next, earning a meal and a bed for one night only, by carrying out some menial task at the institution. The law forbade then to stay for more than one night, thus spreading the burden between the various authorities. By the thirties the structure and purpose of the workhouse expanded to use as a hospital. The 'Muni' provided employment to locals and in one case, to someone destined to be famous: From 1930, for almost ten years, the manageress of the Hastings Municipal Hospital laundry was Catherine McMullen, who on marriage to a Hastings headmaster in 1940 became Catherine Cookson, of eventual world wide literary fame. When shown the slums of Old Town Hastings in the thirties Catherine said that she thought the living conditions superior to those she had left behind in her Northern hometowns, but added perhaps it was the sea breezes that created an illusion of freshness. The workhouse facilities of the hospital were still in use in the early 1940s, although by then most of its inmates were permanent, being sick or disabled. The hospital was closed in 1994 and stood empty for several years, repeatedly falling victim to vandals and arsonists, until it was demolished to make way for a 36-property housing estate. The only original hospital building that remains is on the eastern side of Frederick Road, now converted, to quote the sales literature, 'Frederick Mews, a listed building, tastefully converted into two, three and four-bed roomed terraced houses, with neat front gardens and parking bays'.

HAZEL JONES' FAMILY MEMORIES OF ORE AND THE RIDGE

When Hazel's parents were children they lived at opposite ends of the Ridge but went to the same school in Ore Village; her father lived at Landsview, a house near Lavender Cottage and her mother lived at High Bank, overlooking the Union Workhouse. Hazel's paternal grandmother was a dressmaker and one of her tasks was to make the habits for the nuns at the nearby convent of Holmhurst St Mary at Baldslow Village. She may well have been the dressmaker to whom Emilie refers in her letters. Hazel's maternal uncle, Tom Blackman, contributed an account of his early life to the book, Hastings Voices. He was born in 1913 and lived in High Bank, Ore from the age of two. Hazel remembers her uncle making the nets that he described in the book, 'They were very long and as he worked on them he spread them up the front passage of the cottage, folded over and over again. Sometimes he would make net shopping bags of orange coloured string for my mother and me. Tom learned his net making from his father who was the son of a fisherman. The nets were vital in the practice of rabbit catching in the rural area that surrounded Ore Village; this gave an income when times were particularly hard, most notably during the depression. Tom said that catching rabbits, although illegal was looked upon by the people as almost an honourable profession, like smuggling in the 1700s. When rabbit catchers appeared in court, their offence was described not as poaching but more correctly as 'trespass in search of coney'. Tom did not have a regular job in the 1930s and took on any occupation that would earn money; stoking the boiler in the Parker Road wash house, working in the laundry or on the delivery vans. He slogged as a sawyer, hand cutting through massive elms and oaks or did the back breaking work of turf-laying for two and six (twelve and a half pence) per day. He looked after the rubbish tip at Bulverhythe for eleven pence (four and a half pence) per hour. At the tip a huge hole was being filled with the boulders and clay that were being dug out of the St Leonards seafront for the footings of the modernistic Marine Court apartment building. A long period of unemployment followed so Tom made money here and there, catching shrimps and prawns and gathering mushrooms. In early 1939 he got a job with the railway as a plate-layer, and acting ganger. Eventually, Tom became the railway's vermin destroyer, where his former experience as a rabbit catcher stood him in good stead. In later years ill-health obliged him to take the job of relief gate-keeper at Doleham halt. Hazel Jones said that while on this lonely duty her Uncle Tom made tufted rugs on canvas with the yarn from unravelled knitting. An American tourist was most taken with the designs and wanted to buy them. Tom Blackman's family knew him as a reserved man who rarely spoke about himself and they had no idea he had told his story to the Local History Group for the book. His family learned more from the book than they had ever known about him in his lifetime; Tom died before the book was published.

ORE BRICK FIELDS

Jill Burrows, who has family connections with Ore Village, recounted stories she had heard from them: 'My mother was born in Hastings in April 1931 and some of her family still live there. My grandfather, Mr Pratt, worked at the brick field in Rock Lane before the war and I have very clear memories of the derelict site of the brick fields as a young child, as my Uncle and Aunt moved into a house opposite them in Rock Lane when I was about 7 years old. My grandfather's contribution to the war effort in the early days was, I understand, to help in stripping Hastings Pier of its decking, to prevent the enemy from landing. I also learned that my grandfather was responsible for extinguishing the brick kilns in Rock Lane, when war broke out - apparently to continue brick production would have contravened the blackout regulations. At the beginning of the war my mother's family was living at Pigeon Cove in Rock Lane but later lived in Coghurst Road, prior to moving to Bedfordshire when my mother was evacuated. The field by the brick works was a favourite play spot for local children and the giant chimney of the kiln was a landmark that could be seen from miles around and locals were sad to see it go when it was demolished. Having helped to remove the woodwork from the pier my grandfather was assigned a role in the coastal defences and according to the older members of the family gave horrific accounts of having to take shelter during bombing raids by lying between the gravestones in some of the churchyards along the coast - I believe that most of these were in the Romney Marsh area'.

Vi Pratt, Jill's aunt, aged 80, still lives in Rock Lane, Ore, near the former brick fields; in fact her house is built of the bricks that were made there. Vi was a Land Army girl during the war, work she thoroughly enjoyed. Initially she was sent to Peacehaven and lodged at the Gracie Fields' Orphanage but the star wanted to use the home again for the children so Vi was sent back to live with her family at their Calvert Road home, in Hastings. She then worked on Godden's Farm, growing vegetables. The farm is now the site of the Broomgrove Housing Estate; Godden's Farm fields extended to the area that is now the electricity sub-station, on the corner of the Ridge and Ivyhouse Lane. Vi recalls that standing at the rear of Simes, the metal works on the Ridge, there was a little hut, where they would sit to eat their lunch or shelter from bad weather.

CHURCH STREET.

Behind the parade of shops in Ore Village there is a deep wooded valley; running along its edge and parallel with the back gardens of Greville Road there is a narrow, grass track, where almost nothing remains to indicate that this was once a thriving, residential road called Church Street. It is doubtful that Emilie Crane's visits to the shops in the village ever took her to this street but it was still a thriving community during her residence in the locality and its occupants were certainly regular customers at the local shops. Today, the only sign of there having been a Church Street are a few granite kerbstones, almost covered by soil and weeds. Tangled in overgrown vegetation and mature trees on the steep sided valley are privet and red, rambling roses, the last relics of once well-kept gardens and allotments. The area is now a haven for urban wildlife; owls, foxes and badgers, which have spread their occupancy into nearby gardens, including my own. I have had worse neighbours! Ore is a densely built up part of Hastings and this end of the Ore Valley provides a refreshing area of green among the busy streets. In August 2005 the valley came under threat from developers and thanks to the prompt and concerted efforts of the local community the plan for unsuitable housing was rejected, for the time being. Certainly no such consideration as local opposition was taken into account in the 19th century, when Church Street was built. The first record of a Church Street with property on it is on an Ordnance Survey Map, dated 1873, showing a row of houses. By the 1870s, Ore Village was developing rapidly; many families had moved in from outlying rural areas in the hope of finding work in Hastings, which was on the brink of a boom. At that time, there was a wide chasm between the rich and poor of the locality. Wealthy families owned large, detached houses on The Ridge and in country lanes just outside Ore, while the poor occupied humble, overcrowded homes, which in most cases, had no running water.

Church Street was perhaps the poorest of all the new communities; its residents were mainly labourers and their families. In hard times they made their living as best they could; some, who had come from farming backgrounds used Ore's proximity to the rural area to work in the hop fields and sometimes resorted to poaching, as Magistrates' Court records reveal. Church Street was home to many widows and unmarried mothers, who earned their living as charwomen, laundresses and ironers. It is possible they found jobs at the Union Workhouse, which stood at the end of Church Street. The awareness of the contrast between their own poverty and the orderly sufficiency of the workhouse must have increased their sufferings.

There was a Ragged School in Church Street; these schools were so nicknamed because the children were very badly clothed. These schools were established for children whose families could not afford to pay for their education. The Church Street School was run by a Miss St Paul; she must have been a very kindly lady, for in 1873 she invited her pupils, along with children from the workhouse, to a treat in the garden of her home at Fairlight. This was surely a tremendous event in the Church Street children's lives. They were often underfed, without proper clothing and had no footwear, which was a frequent excuse for not attending school. The children were also expected to add to the family income by going hop-picking or gathering wild produce from fields and hedgerows, for the family table or to sell. Stealing to relieve want was commonplace.

Few records exist of the daily lives of these early, Church Street residents; they were considered to be too lowly to be of any account. No doubt their lives fell into the same mould as those of the many other poor families of Ore; a strong community spirit, the crushing poverty, temporarily obliterated by alcohol, the effect of which often led to street fights, documented in the Magistrates' and local newspaper reports of the day. Qualified medical care was a luxury; local, elderly women were called in to attend to routine ailments and childbirth. Infant mortality was still pitifully high. Well into the 20th century, the Church Street families were still at the lower end of the income scale and ownership of a camera was unheard of, so there are no available photographic records but the grandchildren and children of the early occupants of the forgotten houses have provided memories of life in Church Street.

Former Church Street resident, Fred Cornelius said," See them great trees down there in the valley? When I played down there as a kid they were no thicker than my thumb. We used to have big fights with the boys from Sandown, we used to chase them down the valley and back over the bridge across the stream. The best fights were on the bit of ground called The Green at the bottom of Church Street."

Fighting must have been a significant part of the children's street lives and Angie, who married Peter Quinnell from a Church Street family and still lives in Ore Village said that one of the street's girls was a ferocious fighter. "She would pull out lumps of hair and you could see kids walking about with bald patches". Angie said that even in the 1940s Church Street families were very poor. She went on to say, " But

I could never understand why they pulled the houses down, they were sturdy and well built, maybe it was because they had outside toilets, but a lot of other houses were still like that in the fifties". The Church Street children must have been notorious for their fighting. A child from a neighbouring street said, "I was forbidden to have anything to do with the children from Church Street, they were considered to be far too rough as playmates for a nice little girl!" A Mrs Grace Hayward, born in 1914, speaks in the book, Hastings Voices, published in 1982. She said, "There was such snobbery then, even among the workers. Those who lived in a certain part of Sandown and Church Street were looked down on and you did not play with them; the boys got into trouble and were chased by the police". She could not resist adding, "Those boys were fascinating!" Wally Cornelius, who was a fish hawker for Ore Village for 44 years, said his grandmother lived in Church Street.. He said, " Everyone was hard up then, I used to take my granny a bucket full of gurnards, it's a red, ugly looking fish and nobody wanted to buy it in those days, but it is very tasty. My granny would make what she called 'gurnit pie', it was very good".

Angie Quinnell, who has lived all her life in a house in Victoria Avenue, recounted her memories of local characters and childhood street games in the 1940s. "Charlie Tapp, who now lives in Clifton Road, kept pigs on a slope in Greystone Lane, an unmade track, which overlooks the Church Street valley, where he also grew lots of vegetables. Dick Barton, who used to live on The Ridge, came round every evening on his bike, to switch on the street lamp; he did this with a long wooden stick, which had a hook on the end. The naughty boys would climb up the lamppost and switch it off after he had gone. On Sunday mornings a man called Jack Peters would walk his pig for exercise around the street, keeping it line by patting it on either side with stick. There was a rag and bone man who came round with his cart; if you gave him some rags he would give you a day-old chick. There were street singers, singing all the old songs for money or food. There was one old man who used to walk the streets picking up cigarette ends out of the gutter to re-roll them. It was awful but he was so desperate. There was a great banjo player, Mr Cobby, who was responsible for making huge bonfire guys. They were so big that they had to be fixed to the back of a lorry with very strong wires; sometimes their heads had to be removed so that they could pass beneath overhead cables. Children got aboard the lorry and rode round with the guys. These were made to look like Guy Fawkes must have done, with a buckle on his hat, big high boots and a ruffle round his neck; they were really well made. People worked for months to build these fabulous guys. Then they were burned on a huge bonfire in a field, known as Kemp's Field, at the top of Rock Lane. There were wonderful firework displays too. We played with wooden tops and sticks; the sticks had a leather strip attached, to form a whip. We wound the leather tightly round the top, which had a pointed base, then we pulled it and the top would spin very fast; you kept the top going by whipping it. We used to draw pretty designs on the top with coloured pencils. We had little white clay bubble-pipes; mother would make us up a mug of soapy water with Bibby soap. This was all right, as long as you remembered to blow and not suck, it tasted horrible! The boys were always playing marbles. I had a wonderful collection myself, but I was caught in the playground, playing marbles with a boy instead of doing my lesson and the teacher confiscated my marbles. I never got them back; I didn't dare tell my parents, as my father, Mr Ted Grey was the local policeman. He later became a teacher. When I was a child, you were lucky to see a car pass by for at least an hour, so we were able to have a skipping rope across the road. The whole street would join in. We also played a game called Kick the Can. An empty pea tin would be filled up with small stones; the can was then flattened to keep the stones inside. It would be thrown down the street and one person would hare to get it and then walk backwards, shaking the tin, whilst the other children went and hid. To win the game you had to try, one-by-one, to get the tin, which had been stood in the street. We were constantly moaned at because of the noise but that did not stop us."

Terry Hobbs, now living in Australia, recounted some childhood memories of Church Street: 'My family lived there for maybe two or three years. I could have only been around five or six years old at the time and as I recall it, it wasn't a happy street. There seemed to be a lot of friction between families, whether it was due to the war or not I don't know. We were a family of six, Mum Dad and four boys. We lived at No.76, which was the second block of houses down the left hand side of the street, an end house. There was a pedestrian arch further up on the opposite side that led through to Greville Rd. On a return visit to England some four years ago I found that it was still there. My eldest brother took me there to see it as it is now. Church Street was very stony, it was never surfaced; it always appeared to me in a Z shape. I suppose the war made things difficult, I remember playing in the back yard while the bombs were dropping over the Clive Vale area, landing in Alfred, Canute, and Berlin Roads. A Mr. Patterson lived next door to us, further up was the Blackman family, they had a son called George and I believe he was tragically killed. Above them was our little sweet shop where Mrs Noakes, we nick-named her 'Knocker Noakes', used to serve us from those very large sweet jars. When we entered the shop the old bell would ring on the back of the door. There was one of those swinging cigarette signs that hung outside the shop advertising: 'Woodbines 5 for 2d, 10 for 4d'. A Mrs Payne also lived in this block and she had a daughter named Cathy. Further up after a gap was the Booth & Son family, they owned a kind of wood yard; they were also very clever in making flower arrangements and wreaths. At the top of the street was a set of steps leading into Victoria Avenue, with a stony road on the left, into the top of Greville Rd. Granny Scrace was also living somewhere near us, I knew her quite well in later years when she lived at 3, Victoria Ave.

Down beyond our house was a steep valley we called the "Oller ". On the left of the street, in the hollow, was a large shed like a saw mill and on some days they used to cut up logs. The hollow was a kids' playground, where we slid down the wet slopes on our backsides. There were lots of allotments in that valley, which led into Sandown School in School Rd. There was an Ack-Ack gun situated above the hollow by the dairy opposite Ken Apps' cycle shop. It was a known fact that the gun crews would enjoy watching the kids fighting in Church Street. It was like a war zone between the kids at the top and the bottom of the street. Towards the end of Church Street there was always the aroma of Gurr's Cake shop; if you had the money you could buy an oblong cake for 3d, or the lovely round bread pudding for one and a half pennies. Unfortunately, there were a lot of mice running around in the shop. There was an off-license at the far end of the street, on the corner of Clifton Road. They had one of those pin boards, where you had to push through a pin to win a prize. I can just remember the war effort, when a massive pile of anything made of metal was collected on what we called the Green; I believe a newspaper photograph was taken of this event.' (It was; a copy of the photo is published in my book Letters to Hannah. A second photo taken by the local paper of the event provided the picture of Church Street boys, George and Leslie Potter, in this book.)

Like so many buildings in Hastings and St Leonards, Church Street was scheduled for demolition as part of the great post-war effort to create a 'New Britain'. On 10th October 1959 the Hastings and St Leonards Observer carried the announcement. "In a report on clearance areas, the Public Hygiene Committee, acting on representations by the Medical Officer of Health, Dr T H Parkman, are recommending to the Town Council in respect of demolition of the following properties, which are unfit for habitation for reason of their bad arrangement or the narrowness and/or bad arrangement of the streets, dangerous or injurious to the health of the inhabitants; thirty-five houses in Church Street" . In 1964, less than a hundred years after it was built, a whole street in Ore Village disappeared. The families were re-housed round the town, some on the then brand new Broomgrove Council Estate, just off the long road, The Ridge.

PART FOUR

EMILIE AND ME

Emilie Crane and the letters that she sent from Lavender Cottage changed my life. Emilie's letters came into my hands via my family's Hastings website message board, after Canadian Wendy Johnson posted an enquiry there to ask if a house, called Lavender Cottage, on The Ridge, Hastings, still existed. Wendy's message explained that she owned a collection of letters, written from Lavender Cottage to her Aunt Marion, in Canada by her English cousin Miss Emilie Crane, during and after WWII. Emilie's correspondence covered a 13 year period: The letters began as thanks for food parcels but over the years they created a picture of the daily lives of the aging Emilie and her two similarly elderly house companions and of a small seaside town enduring and recovering from six years of war.

I emailed Wendy a photograph of Lavender Cottage and she posted to me photocopies of the letters, giving me her permission to use them as I wished. The parcel of letters arrived in May 2001 but their close reading was set aside for a while, as most of my spare time was taken up with researching and writing a good news column for my family's Hastings website. The site came about as a result of my children teaching me to use a computer in May 1999, my sixty-fifth year, with my retirement imminent, from my job with a Hastings language school. I was not a very apt computer student but my family's patience paid off and within a few months I was reasonably computer literate and a daily Internet user. To use my new-found enthusiasm my family suggested we combine their technological skills and my writing abilities to create a few pages for a website about Hastings.

I retired from employment in September 1999 and immediately embarked on the research for the Hastings website. In 1999 anything related to the Internet still created excitement and I was warmly welcomed everywhere. Due to my former job with the language school, I was already familiar with the local tourist attractions and events but I decided to approach my research on Hastings and St Leonards like a stranger, looking anew at its every aspect. It was an exciting and rewarding four months and the new site, already surpassing a few pages, was quietly launched on 21st December 1999. To keep the site lively, new features were regularly introduced; pages on Hastings' long-past, modern and WWII history, information for overseas students and a comprehensive guide to entertainments, a page for every pub in the town and weekly-updated 'good news' pages. The website's content, which included a collection of local photographs, taken by the family, eventually became a comprehensive guide to Hastings and St Leonards for holiday makers, visitors and existing and would-be residents.

To introduce an element of fun we invented a feature called 'Ask Harold', dealing with questions specifically about Hastings. To provide a face for the feature, a young, male family friend was persuaded to put on a vaguely Saxon fancy dress costume and pose for photographs at Hastings Castle, as 'King Harold.' Before long teachers were using the site as a regular classroom resource and 'Harold', (in fact me,) was bombarded with questions about the Battle of Hastings and local history. 'Harold' eventually won his own question and answer column in 'Homes', the Sussex property magazine. Gathering local news stories increased my knowledge of the sunnier side of Hastings' life and the town's festivals, functions and special events gave me plenty to write about. I also found a steady supply of 'human stories', as well as commenting, tongue in cheek, on the curious machinations of Hastings Borough Council. Our website eventually amounted to over 1000 pages. By doing all the varied work for the website, I was unwittingly getting an informal course in the skills I would need for preparing the book I would one day write.

As a result of looking for local news I met Joyce Brewer, Ivor White and Noel Care, people who eventually became contributors to my books and also friends. I was introduced to Joyce when I was looking for somebody with an interest in the wildlife of the Broomgrove Valley, to help with a news story: Badgers and protected species of lizard in the valley were under threat from developers. Joyce has been a resident of Broomgrove for most of her life and has a special concern for the flora and fauna of the valley. As soon as I met her I was taken by her sense of humour and honesty. I learned during our chat that Joyce has a great interest in the local, home front history of WWII and she loves writing so she agreed to record her wartime memories for the website's modern history section.

Ivor White first came to my notice in a local newspaper article, in which he said he wanted to meet Lord Richard Attenborough, who was to visit Hastings on 22nd October 2001 for a special preview of his film, Grey Owl. When Ivor was demobilized from wartime service in the Irish Guards in 1948, he took employment as projectionist at the Hastings Ritz Cinema. There Ivor met the young Attenborough, when he made a personal appearance at Hastings Ritz Cinema to promote the film, The Winslow Boy, in which he starred. Richard and Ivor were photographed together in the cinema projection room. Ivor wanted a chance to meet Lord Attenborough again and to give him a copy of the vintage photograph. As I had a ticket to the pre-performance lunch and the film's screening of Grey Owl, I was able to arrange a brief meeting between the two men in the foyer of the St Mary in the Castle Art Centre, where the lunch was held. Ivor said that it was quite a moving encounter for him and that Lord Attenborough is every bit the endearing 'luvvie' he appears to be in interviews. After his job at the cinema Ivor moved on to a career as a freelance newspaper photographer. A widower at aged 74, Ivor taught himself to use a computer and build websites. He is unfailingly helpful to me with his photographic and technological skills and has also contributed many accounts of his wartime experiences to my books.

Noel Care responded to my request for people to recount their wartime experiences for the Hastings website. Noel was a teenaged civil defence worker in Hastings during the war and like Joyce Brewer, a good writer. He, too, contributed many chapters of his wartime experiences to the website. Sadly, he was seriously disabled by a stroke in December 2001, before he could finish his writings. At one time Joyce and Noel's memories were listed among the best Internet sources for eye-witness home front WWII history and their writings now appear in my books.

During the summer of 2001 Wendy Johnson and I emailed each other frequently, discussing Emilie Crane's letters. Wendy found some photographs of Lavender Cottage, taken in 1950 and a picture of

Emilie, the first we had ever seen of her. In September I obtained a copy of Emilie Crane's death certificate and this document made her seem more real to me. During the darkening autumn evenings I began to re-read more closely the hundreds of pages of Emilie's long-ago postings to Canada. I thought for the first of many times that I wished I had known her; a feeling often expressed later by her 'fans'. Emilie's final, sad letters, written in the months before her death, reduced me to tears. I felt strongly that the letters must be made into a book. At the start of 2002 I began to transcribe Emilie's letters, as well as continuing to research and write the Hastings website's weekly news pages. Emilie's letters made fascinating reading but to become a book they needed something more to support them. I gave the letters to my 24 year-old daughter-in-law, Angelique, for her opinion. Within a few days she had read them and told me that she had become drawn into Emilie's life and felt very sad when learning of the old lady's lonely death. She had also found the letters interesting and thought-provoking. Over the next few weeks she asked me many questions about WWII and the long period of austerity that followed and this inspired me and the notion of the 'Dear Angelique' part of Letters from Lavender Cottage was conceived.

On 26th March 2002 Wendy Johnson, an Anglophile and a regular visitor to the UK, paid a first visit to Hastings with her husband Walter and their 29 year old daughter, Heather. It was almost a year since Wendy had first contacted the website and during that time we had come to know each other through our emails. When I went to meet Wendy and her family at Hastings Station I felt rather nervous; it's not everybody who takes kindly to a stranger probing into their family history, but I realised from her warm greeting that my anxiety was unfounded. The main destinations of the day were the places mentioned in Emilie's letters, the most important of which for Wendy was Lavender Cottage, several miles from the centre of Hastings. Until she saw the cottage I had not understood the emotional connection Wendy felt with the place. She told me recently: "You know that I was moved to tears when I stood in front of Lavender Cottage for the first time. Had the book not been written I would have been interested to see where an ancestor had lived, but growing to know and love Emilie as the book progressed brought it all alive for me, as it did for many others."

After Wendy's visit I felt enthused and I re-read Emilie's letters, making notes on every reference to national and local affairs, also bearing in mind the questions Angelique had asked about the period. Many of her questions related to food; rationing and the shortage of almost everything that featured strongly in Emilie's letters. I began to research contemporary news archives for information on home front and post war events that had previously made only a passing impression on my childhood consciousness; this research became a re-living of my own past.

In April 2002 I started to study the archive of The Hastings and St Leonards Observer at Hastings Reference Library, to find news items that related to the local events to which Emilie referred in her letters. The period of bi-weekly visits to the library was a happy interlude and an experience I was pleased to repeat for my following books about the social history of WWII Hastings. The research help from the staff at the reference library is always very good. They also manage a busy, pay-by-the-hour Internet access service, as well as many telephone and personal callers. Hastings library is housed in the Brassey Institute, an imposing town house, built by Lord Brassey for his family in 1888 and later donated to Hastings as a museum. It is probably not a particularly convenient building as far as the staff is concerned but I have grown fond of its reference room, with high ceilings and arched windows. Researchers sit at broad conference tables, together with the lonely and elderly, who still go to reference libraries to find warmth and to use the daily newspapers as a screen behind which to doze. Characters began to emerge; one in particular is a retired mechanical engineer, who visits the library to read the magazine, The New Scientist, on Friday mornings. He seems to find much on the magazine's letters page to reduce him to stifled laughter. Sometimes the letters are so hilarious to him that he is moved to share their contents with others seated at the research table or with the staff. Another regular rips his notes into small fragments and mixes them with discarded sweet wrappers and unwanted leaflets, in a messy drift across the research table. Head-mistressy reprimands by a stern librarian make no difference to his behaviour - perhaps he enjoys them! There are the sniffers, to whom I long to hand a tissue, the snorers and the grunters. Groups of chattering, overseas students and argumentative asylum-seekers arrive at their appointed hour to use the computers. Whatever happened to the 'shushing' of old-time libraries? But in spite of all this I found the atmosphere of the large room comfortingly 'school-ish'. As soon as I opened the worn, leather-bound broadsheet copies of the wartime Hastings and St Leonards Observer all the distractions faded. It is sad to note that these old newspapers, printed on inferior wartime paper, are now crumbling to pieces. After using them, one's lap and the surrounding floor are littered with flakes of yellowed newsprint. I am told that the local news for the WWII and post-war period is not preserved in any other format and these deteriorating copies are the only record of the town's news for those years. Here is a conflict between accessibility and preservation and I fear that within the foreseeable future this archive will be beyond use.

During the summer months of 2002 the background research into Emilie's life took shape, and it is thanks to her that my interest in Hastings World War Two home front social history was fired. The work of compiling and writing the material to enlarge upon Emilie Crane's letters from Lavender Cottage was completed by the end of August. During that month Angelique told me that she was expecting her first child, my fourth grandchild. Angelique had offered to proof read the book for me but she was not feeling well and I thought the work was an imposition. Proof reading is not easy, as the following passage demonstrates:

Aoccdrnig to a rscheearch sdtuy at Cmabrigde Uinervtisy, it deosn't mttaer in waht oredr the ltteers in a wrod are, the olny iprmoatnt tihng is taht the frist and lsat ltteer be at the rghit pclae. The rset can be a ttoal mses and you can sitll raed it wouthit a porbelm. Tihs is bcuseae the huamn mnid deos not raed ervey lteter by istlef, but the wrod as a wlohe.

Wendy Johnson volunteered to proof read Letters from Lavender Cottage and thanks to the Internet, the manuscript was transmitted in seconds by email and likewise the return of her corrections. Wendy was helped in the work with a further proof reading by her mother, Eleanor Russell. It was at about this time that my family decided our Hastings website would have to be brought to a close. It was taking up so much of our time and not a little money and all of our lives were going in new and busy directions. I wrote my last news items for the site in the first week of September 2002, with feelings of regret and relief.

While writing Letters from Lavender Cottage I had been thinking about how to find a publisher for it; my initial enquiries were not encouraging. Since the home computer revolution, books are being written in the hundreds of thousands, all over the world. One statistic said that in the UK alone 340 books are released for every day of the year; that includes Sundays. I then came across the disheartening phrase, 'slush pile'. This is where unsolicited manuscripts are put on their arrival in a publisher's office. I was told that if you are very lucky, one of the staff readers may pick up a manuscript from the slush pile and give it a cursory glance. Sometimes they may read a few pages but it is very rarely that a book gets further reading or is considered for publication. Seeking publishing ideas, I went on to look at books by local authors and saw that in some cases they were published by the writer. I contacted two of these to ask how it is done and I am grateful to Sussex history writers Geoff Hutchinson and Peter Longstaff-Tyrell for the advice they gave me. Geoff advised me about marketing methods and Peter put me in touch with a local printer, John Davis, who was among the earliest in Hastings and St Leonards to be offering a print-on-demand service for authors' books. John guided me through the process of preparing the book for printing and by the 8th October 2002 I had my first properly bound, draft copies of Letters from Lavender Cottage but I still had not found a way to promote the book.

In the summer of 2002, I had spent an afternoon being interviewed by BBC Southern Counties Radio presenter Neil Pringle, when he was making sound recordings for a new series called 'A Sense of Place', about people who lived in Sussex and Kent communities. He was very interested in our Hastings website and asked me to let him know if I came across any suitable stories for his regular morning show. It occurred to me that the story of how I came to write a book based on the Lavender Cottage letters might be regarded as a good subject for an interview. I rang the studio and spoke to Neil's researcher, who asked me to send her a copy of Letters from Lavender Cottage. After a few days the studio contacted me to say that they would like to do a live interview with me about the book, from the Hastings Southern Counties Radio location studio and link it with a live interview with Wendy from London, who was visiting the UK with her husband. Wendy was excited to hear that she was to broadcast from the iconic Broadcasting House. In Hastings, the day of the interview was one of squally rain and wind and the town centre, where the location studio is situated, was not the best place to go. The interview was scheduled for 10.20am and I arrived at ten o'clock; the studio was unstaffed and entry gained by punching numbers in a security pad. I pushed the buttons but there was no response from the lock - it had been vandalised. I rang the BBC studio staff in Guildford and they made several attempts to open the door from there, with eventual success. I finally got into the cramped studio at fifteen minutes past ten. The rain, gale and panic had rendered me drenched and breathless and I was just about to speak to thousands of people on the radio! I crammed the headphones on my wet, tangled hair and immediately heard Neil Pringle announcing the next record and the upcoming item about the book. The interview began on time: He asked me how I had come into possession of the letters and why I had written the book and Wendy was also questioned about her part in the story. I did not know it at the time but she too had been going through her own drama at Broadcasting House. She later told me: "I arrived at the prestigious address and was ushered into a small, scruffy studio and told to put on headphones and not to touch anything. I was supposed to join in the interview when I heard Neil Pringle start to talk. Unfortunately, at the time the interview was to start, all I could hear was Harry Belafonte singing. It was extremely frustrating to know that I had come all the way from Canada and probably wouldn't even be heard. Then in the distance I could hear Victoria's voice, and in a few more minutes was able to join in the interview. When we heard the finished version we found it had all gone quite well considering the hassle it had been, both at my end and in Hastings for Victoria as well. My only regret was that I had to return the security badge I had been given. I wanted a souvenir of this special day". Friends who had heard the transmission said how smooth and professional Wendy and I sounded. (This reminded me of the analogy of the swan, calmly gliding across a lake while its feet paddle like mad)!

It was a complete surprise when at the start of the interview Neil announced that an excerpt from Letters from Lavender Cottage would be read. The reading opened with ambient music, and Emilie Crane's first letter, dated 1942, was spoken by an older lady, with just the right kind of voice. She read...

"Lavender Cottage, June 9th 1942.

My Dear Marion,
I can't tell you how delighted I was to receive your lovely parcel this morning; it was a welcome surprise and more than kind of you to send it. My best thanks to you. I don't know how you came to choose the things most needed and such acceptable items. I think the things we have most missed here are butter and fruit; all the fats are so scarce and the rations do not allow us much, so we shall revel in nice bread and butter. As for oranges, the small consignment sent over is reserved for children under six, which is as it should be, therefore, we shall rejoice in the fruit juice.

The tea will be a treat; I gave my ration coupons to Miss Marriott, who can only drink china tea. I am very intrigued with the egg powder and shall try it at the first opportunity. I have scoured Hastings for a saucepan cleaner, how did you think of that? Soap and sugar are of course rationed strictly. I can get saccharine but I do not care much for it; such sickly stuff. The serviettes will be very useful as the paper shortage is acute. Hence the notepaper I am using, taken from some old volumes, from a period when they used better paper than they do now.

I do hope the above remarks do not sound as if we are in a bad way; it is only that things are in short supply. We do miss some things, naturally, but we expect that in a terrible war. I think the light is beginning to come through at last, don't you? Hitler is not having a very pleasant time. All day the fighters and bombers go over us on their way to France and Germany. They are Canadian, American, British and Polish forces; we know they do some damage. We have had two raids recently and there were a good many casualties. But everyone here is wonderfully cheerful and none doubt of ultimate victory. We had an exciting time last week when the wounded from the

Commando raid on France were brought to the hospital here; I am sorry to say that one died.

I wish I could do more to help but my age, 71, is against it. I took the first aid course and went to help in a First Aid Post but it was so damp I got pleurisy and the doctor would not let me go there again. So I went for an anti-gas course and received a certificate but fortunately the Germans have not resorted to gas. I offered myself for clerical work but they wanted younger people, so I fell back on door-to-door collecting for the National Savings Campaign and that has been successful. The garden is a great joy and we really have done well with vegetables but fruit is very shy and does not like the cold climate up here.

There is little news to give you and each day is the repetition of another; planes overhead, air raid alerts and wireless news. Please give my love to everyone and much to yourself, with renewed thanks,

Yours affectionately

Emilie. PS this letter is a scrawl but the paper is not easy to write on."

I was grateful for the care that Southern Counties had taken to present my piece and more so when the encouraging emails and book orders started to arrive, via the new website that my family had constructed for Letters from Lavender Cottage. Wendy and Walter came down to Hastings from London the next day and we had a celebratory lunch with Joyce Brewer, Ivor White and some members of my family. Wendy is a very keen quilter and to commemorate the publication of Letters from Lavender Cottage she presented me with a quilted picture of the cottage. She later stitched a duplicate for herself, which hangs in her home, near her computer. In the weeks leading up to Christmas the sales of my book really took off: "They are flying off the shelves", they told me in Hastings' Olio Bookshop. The owners of this, Hastings last family-run bookshop, Mr and Mrs Rees and their staff are great supporters of local writers and the shop itself is a centre for interesting conversations, literary and otherwise.

My being given a radio interview emboldened me and I asked the county newspaper, The Argus and the glossy, regional magazine, Sussex Life if they would be interested in covering the story of the book. They both agreed and in December 2002 the Argus did a half page article, with a photo of me outside Lavender Cottage. Sussex Life allocated four pages, (four pages!) of their Christmas edition to Letters from Lavender Cottage, including quotes from Emilie's letters and my biography.

A few weeks after Letters from Lavender Cottage went on sale I began to get letters and emails from its readers, who were entranced by Emilie Crane, the book's real life heroine:-

Dear Mrs Seymour,
I have just this minute finished Letters from Lavender Cottage. I wish I could talk to you, face-to-face, to tell you how much I absolutely loved it. Emilie's letters were so wonderfully descriptive and I ached for her when her time at the Cottage was drawing to a close and then came the end. What an incredibly brave lady she was and always able to look on the bright side when all about her was falling apart. Your narrative was a perfect complement.
J M Canada

Dear Victoria,
I felt I just had to drop you an E-mail after reading your excellent book 'Letters from Lavender Cottage' which I enjoyed tremendously. I bought it as a Christmas present. As it was a gift for someone else my first intention was to do nothing more than just read a few pages to satisfy my curiosity but I found by Boxing Day I had completely finished it, being unable to put it down. After reading the book I had a good feeling that has stayed with me over Christmas and well into the New Year.
J L. Eastbourne.

Dear Victoria,
I wanted to thank you for writing such a lovely book as Letters from Lavender Cottage. I thought it was remarkable how these elderly

ladies not only took care of each other but so many other people who lived nearby. It seems that it was a special time - people were more caring of each other. Thank you again for a most delightful book.
M W. U S A.

Other correspondents asked if I knew anything more about Emilie's life; the aim of this second book about Lavender Cottage has been to address that question.

In October 2002 I asked the Hastings and St Leonards Observer if they would cover the story of Letters from Lavender Cottage. The Observer photo shoot was arranged to take place in the Hastings Museum, where there was an exhibition of home front WWII memorabilia on display. Unfortunately, when the photographer and I arrived, the exhibition was packed with a group of school children and we had to go outside the entrance to take the picture. My chief recollections of the event are that just as the photographer took his shot a squirrel leapt over my feet, with a ginger cat in hot pursuit and the simultaneous emergence from the building of the children, who resorted to the idiotic behaviour that seems standard in teenagers these days on glimpsing a media camera. Christmas came and went and the photograph and the press release I had submitted about my book were unpublished. Never-the-less, Letters from Lavender Cottage was selling very well and the thought of its having been a Christmas gift to hundreds of people was very pleasant. After Christmas, I contacted Meridian Television, who arranged to film me on the morning of 7th January 2003. In spite of the roads being very icy, Meridian's TV journalist, Paul Fitzgerald arrived at my house on time, along with a camera man and sound technician, all three in separate cars, one loaded with equipment. I imagined that this mass arrival of a TV crew might be the cause of some speculation among the neighbours. Possibly they thought, "She's had a lottery win!" The small dining room in my two-up two-down, mid-terrace cottage was swamped with TV recording and lighting equipment. We spent what was for me an anxious hour on filming the interview, all of us shivering because my noisy gas boiler had to be turned off for the sake of the sound-track. We then drove in convoy to the Ridge, to film outside Lavender Cottage. The roads remained icy and the biting wind made me think of Emilie's frequent references in her letters to the hard winters on the Ridge. For the camera I was instructed to walk past

Joyce Brewer

Ivor White

Noel Care

Wendy Johnson and her mother Eleanor Russell proof read Letters
from Lavender Cottage.

The commemorative quilted picture of Lavender Cottage.

Olio Books, Hastings last family-owned bookshop.

Wendy Johnson records the audio book,
Letters from Lavender Cottage.

Miss Ann Widdecombe MP at the launch of Victoria's book, Court in the Act ~ Crime and Policing in WWII Hastings. November 2004.

Emilie's house, pause, look at it, count to ten and walk on. I had to do this six times, as heavy traffic repeatedly spoiled the shot. In this manner another hour passed. As I stood by the cottage drive I noticed a cluster of snowdrops in bloom on a sheltered grassy bank at the gate. I wondered if Emilie Crane's friend, Clare Marriott, had planted the original bulbs and what the Lavender Cottage ladies would have made of all this media fuss. I was told that the transmission of the interview would be at 6.00pm in the Meridian TV news that evening. It was the last item in the programme and lasted less than two minutes but it was beautifully presented. It seems to me that this is the ratio; two hours of preparation and filming for two or less minutes of screen time. The whole experience brought home to me the power of television. After the transmission, strangers in my community spoke to me, while others, exhibiting typical British reserve, merely gave me a knowing, friendly smile. For a long time after, when I was introduced to new people, some would say, "Oh yes, I saw you on TV; you are the Lavender Cottage Lady".

Wendy Johnson asked me several times during that winter if my local paper had covered the story of Letters from Lavender Cottage yet; they had not. Without my knowing, she wrote to the Observer, taking them to task for "ignoring a local celebrity". The Observer reporter, Ann Terry, rang me to apologise for the paper's oversight and to arrange an interview and another photo shoot. This entailed a third trip to a still chilly Ridge, for some more posing outside Lavender Cottage. (I was told that Letters from Lavender Cottage readers had taken to searching out the location of cottage, to be photographed in front of it, holding up the book). Ann's piece in the Observer on March 14th 2003 gave a further boost in my book's sales. Ann Terry later submitted a re-working of the article about my book to a Hastings Observer publication called Discovering Retirement. The piece was part of an initiative to encourage older people to use the Internet. An article on Ivor White also appeared in the same edition. His headline referred to Ivor as "An Internet Guru at 76", while I was patronised with "Vivacious Grandmother". I should not gripe. The sales for Letters from Lavender Cottage continued steadily and I was very busy writing my second book, Letters to Hannah.

A later piece of publicity for Letters from Lavender Cottage was in the

May 2003 edition of the national magazine, "Yours", aimed at the older generation. The story of how my book came to be written featured in the magazine's promotion called, The Internet Changed My Life. The article, with a photograph of Wendy and me, was only about 200 words long but it included my phone number. Throughout the summer of 2003 I received many phone calls from "Yours" readers, from all over Great Britain. I had some chats with nostalgic former residents of Hastings and heard many stories of personal WWII experiences in other parts of the country. Every caller ordered a copy of Letters from Lavender Cottage.

In the autumn my son and Angelique made a reconnoitre visit to Charing in Kent, to find the crematorium and garden of remembrance, where the ashes of Emilie Crane and her dear friend Clare Marriott were scattered. When they entered the circular garden of remembrance they thought it would be impossible to locate a particular memorial plaque among the thousands that were closely ranged round the enclosing walls. They spent a fruitless hour trying to track down the dedication to Emilie and Clare but finally gave up. Just as they were leaving the garden they spotted Emilie's name. In November Angelique and my son took me to see the plaque, as part of a memory-lane excursion they arranged for me. The first stop was Dover Castle, to see the secret wartime tunnels exhibition. These excavations, deep into the chalk cliffs are entered via a sharply sloping tunnel, lined with corrugated metal sheets. The public is greeted by sound effects of an enemy raid in progress. The din of air raid sirens, anti-aircraft guns, bomb explosions and aircraft engines and the claustrophobic feeling engendered by people shuffling down a narrow tunnel into semi-darkness brought back frightening memories of my childhood experiences of going into an underground shelter. I felt an urge to reach for a reassuring adult hand, forgetting for a moment that I am an old woman now. I did not realise until then how close to the surface are long-ago memories.

The tour of the tunnels was so enthralling that I soon forgot my anxiety, which was further dispelled by a tour of Dover Castle. By the time we got to Charing, dusk was about to fall. A late-in-the-day funeral had just ended and the car park of the crematorium was crowded with posh cars and city-types, dressed in sombre clothes, puffing on much needed cigarettes and chatting in that half-respectful, half-relieved way, which sometimes marks the conclusion of a funeral. I went into the garden and saw Emilie's and Clare's memorial plaque, at the base of a wall, where fading summer flowers still blossomed. In the centre of the gardens, surrounded by a rose bed, stood a fountain, very similar in design to the one in Bessborough Gardens, where Emilie was born. Beyond the garden there was a leafless copse, black against a red sky. I thought of Emilie's comments on the beauty of the setting winter sun, seen from the window of Lavender Cottage, as she wrote her letter to Marion and Beatrice. This plot seemed the perfect last resting place for Emilie Crane.

The companion book to Letters from Lavender Cottage, Letters to Hannah, was officially launched in November 2003 at a tea-party at Hastings' Mount Pleasant Court, in their community room; several of the book's contributors were resident at the flats. I had also invited to the launch all the people who had given me accounts of their wartime experiences for the book. It was a remarkable afternoon - a bringing together of the cast of a real-life drama and a gathering that reunited some friends who had lost touch in the war. How the playwright in Emilie Crane would have loved the occasion.

Whilst I was writing Letters to Hannah it was suggested to me that Letters from Lavender Cottage would make a good audio book. I had no idea how to go about this but talked to Ivor White, who seems to know something about almost everything electronic. He told me that his son Tim, a musician and composer, had a recording studio in his house and he said he would ask him if he would consider helping me with the project. I was impressed with the work that Tim had already done in the field of recording voices. He and his friends had written, produced and recorded a play that won a competition and was broadcast to Hastings on a Christmas radio station called Radio Cracker. I began to believe that with Tim's help it would be possible to make Letters from Lavender Cottage into a talking book but the original manuscript would require considerable abridgement. After the launch of Letters to Hannah I began the editing work on Emilie Crane's story. I decided that the first cuts would be to my own story and after that, to a lesser degree, to Emilie's correspondence. Over eight weeks I reduced the original book to 30,000 words but I calculated it still ran to much more than three hours of talk. And who to do all this talking? I had enjoyed seeing actress Maxine Roach perform at the Stables Theatre in a number of roles and I thought she would be a suitable reader of Emilie's words. Maxine agreed to record the part of Emilie but I agonized over who should read my narrative in the book. My usual listening is to BBC Radio 4, for the most part a spoken word station, so I began to take closer interest in broadcasts of short stories and audio books. Not every reader sounded like a professional performer; in fact, at times, the less 'actor-ish' the reader the more authentic the result. I decided, not without some misgivings, to read the narrative myself. Maxine and I did some test recordings, appreciating Tim's expertise and very up-to-date recording equipment. He taught us how to manage 'fluffs' so that he could edit them out more easily and explained how important it was to record as much as possible at one sitting, as the timbre of the voice changes from day to day. For me, the highlight of the recording sessions was when Wendy Johnson came to Hastings in mid-January in 2004 to record those of the Lavender Cottage letters that were written by her grandmother, who visited Hastings in spring 1955. Tim composed phrases of music to link the scenes and recorded sound effects that created atmosphere and added a piece of Christmas music written by Eleanor Russell. The CD was completed and ready for sale by autumn 2004. The audio book of Letters from Letter to Lavender Cottage was serialised on Hastings' hospital radio in spring 2005. Throughout the year that the audio book was under preparation I was researching and writing my third book, called Court in the Act, a social history of crime and policing in WWII Hastings.

It is not only in giving me the letters and proof reading my manuscripts that Wendy Johnson has played a major part in bringing the story of her cousin Emilie Crane to public attention. She became an informal publicity agent for Letters from Lavender Cottage in her community and on the Internet. She emailed her family, friends and the members of the web groups to which she belongs to tell them about Letters from Lavender Cottage. She sold copies of the book almost anywhere she went. Wendy would strike up conversations with strangers in cafes or elsewhere and chat so enthusiastically about Letters from Lavender Cottage that a book sale could result. She gave talks to women's groups and was asked back to recount the progress of the book. I had become so influenced by the style of Emilie's letters that I found I could write in her manner, so I offered to provide Wendy's audience with a 21st century letter from "Emilie", updating her activities.

Dear Marion and Beatrice,

What an extraordinary time I am having at the moment! I was rather concerned when dear little Wendy sent Victoria the copies of the letters I had written to you both so long ago and I was rather shocked and embarrassed when she turned them into a book. I told myself not to be silly. I thought it unlikely that people would be interested in the ramblings of a nonentity like me but I was completely mistaken. It seems the story of the household at Lavender Cottage and how Clare, Edith and I managed with rationing is very popular. Readers have sent Victoria the kindest of letters, from all over the world, some of them saying pleasant things about me. One young woman referred to the story as 'hauntingly beautiful', a little extreme, my dears, don't you think?

Many people also liked the picture of me on the cover and said that in my floral pinafore and carpet slippers, I reminded them of their elderly aunts or grannies in WWII. This dismayed me somewhat. Had I known this photograph was going to be so widely seen, I would have changed my clothes and combed my hair. But as it was, Clare and I were very excited about actually finding someone to take the photographs at last and we particularly wanted James, our cat, to be shown to advantage, so we forgot about ourselves.

Once I got over the shock of it all, I began to enjoy the excitement. Victoria seems to be having such a wonderful time with the book and she and I have had various adventures together. She is rather pushy but she means well and one must encourage literary endeavour. I am sure that you, Beatrice as a writer, will particularly understand this. To make a short tale of it, Letters from Lavender Cottage is being considered as a talking book. So Victoria has to edit the book and she has no experience of this at all. I said to her: 'Don't worry, it will come, you did not know how to write a book till you met me, did you?

Victoria gave a talk in June about our book, to a women's group, called the Monday Wives. This same group has been meeting on Monday evenings at Hastings All Saints Church Hall for over 30 years. In fact, they used to be called the Young Wives but they felt that as so much time has passed it was time for a name change. Victoria told them the story of our book and afterwards they asked questions for half an hour. Victoria had prepared a display of copies of WWII government pamphlets on matters such as what to do in the event of a German invasion, gas attacks and fire bombing. She also had examples of wartime, home front propaganda posters and a genuine WWII gas mask. Some of the women had been children in the war; I thought the reminiscences would never cease! We both enjoyed the evening immensely. One member of the audience gave Victoria her family's wartime recipe book, ration book and identity card, how kind people are!

Three days later we gave a talk about Hastings in World War Two to a group of adolescent Italian students, in the assembly hall of the Victorian Ore Village School. Victoria spoke slowly and clearly, using her very best English. I had to smile, because it reminded me of my school days. The students were very quiet, so unusual for Latin peoples, but Victoria said to me that perhaps they were falling asleep from boredom! Just think- they were our enemies during the war!

In July we had a delightful excursion. We went to an hotel in the pretty Kent village of Hawkhurst, for a conference and buffet lunch with the Society of Authors. It was an absolutely sweltering day and we journeyed on the top deck of a bus, which afforded the most splendid views of the glorious Sussex and Kent countryside. The lunch company was very impressive: 'Real authors, who have been writing for years', as Victoria said to me later. We chatted with many people; I think they call it networking these days.

We have planned a book-sales stall for Hastings Week, in October. It's at a genealogical fair organized by the Hastings and Rother Family History Society. Victoria has contacted various local history writers and persuaded them to take part, selling their own books, so there will be quite a little gaggle of authors present. Victoria has been working very hard to complete her second book, Letters to Hannah, in which I make a brief appearance; new information about Edith and me has only recently turned up. I won't spoil the surprise!

What a very hot spell we are having at present. I expect the occupants of Lavender Cottage are glad of living at those cooler, 500 feet above sea level. My garden there is still very well looked after and is flourishing; flowers, fruits and vegetables abound; so gratifying. I cannot say, as I so often do, that things are going on as usual, because the idea of 'usual' has completely gone out of the window. No doubt Victoria has more plans to drag us both hither and thither and expose us to all sorts of publicity again, but I must confess that I secretly enjoy it.

Do tell young Wendy I am truly not in the least cross with her about the letters, she has given Victoria and me a new lease of life!

With very much affection to you both,

Cousin Emilie.

"Emilie's" reference to the Society of Authors introduces another person who became influential in my writing career. John Dawes, writer, printer and publisher was made aware of my book by his friend, my printer, John Davis. John Dawes read Letters from Lavender Cottage and he telephoned me, both to congratulate and encourage. It was he who told me about the Society of Authors and his own involvement in it. My attendance as a guest at the society's regional meeting at Hawkhurst was at John Dawes' invitation. This introduction led me to join the society. The self-publishing author should not think they are unsuitable for membership of the society; there is a reduced membership fee for people who do not make very much money from their writing. It is also quietly pleasing to read in the society's membership list the names of famous writers of modern literature and know that one's own name also appears in that list.

During the time that I was still gathering news for our Hastings website in April 2002, a local newspaper article about a TV company visiting Hastings to film a WWII detective series caught my attention. The company, Greenlit Productions, took over the streets of Hastings,

Old Town and the area was closed to pedestrians and cars. As filming began, the entrances to the narrow streets were crammed with spectators, hoping to catch a glimpse of somebody famous, while shopkeepers gazed on glumly, wondering how much business they were losing as a result of street closures. The series was to be called Foyle's War; Michael Kitchen was playing the lead role of Chief Superintendent Inspector Foyle, he was a real-life policeman in WWII who investigated war-related crimes, such as spying and racketeering. Scenes were also shot on Hastings beach, when the 1940 Dunkirk rescue operation was recreated for the second episode. Local fisherman Graham Bossom's fishing boat, the Lady Rose, was used as a Dunkirk rescue vessel and Hastings fishermen had roles as extras. This episode's depiction of wounded and dying British troops returning to Hastings shores was a fiction, as none actually came here, but to see the painful scenes re-enacted with Hastings as a backdrop brought home to me the horror of the real event. Throughout Foyle's War there are many shots of the view over the closely clustered rooftops of Hastings Old Town, its picturesque streets and the tall, black net huts on the beach. One summer afternoon, during a later filming session I went to have a peep at the action. I slipped past the policeman in Croft Road who was holding back cars and pedestrians and I saw the filming of a short segment: A girl in WAAF uniform crossed the road to Foyle's house, as an elderly lady in 1940's dress passed by, wicker shopping basket in hand, like Emilie Crane. I was amused to see that the kerb-side, yellow lines had been painted with adhesive and scattered with what looked like cat-litter, to obscure the modern traffic markings.

Letters from Lavender Cottage was published a few weeks before the first episode of Foyle's War was screened and it was not long before the messages on my book's website began to reflect the connection people were making between Lavender Cottage and Foyle's War. But there was another closer connection with Foyle's War to come: My third book, which I began in early 2004, is Court in the Act ~ Crime and Policing in WWII Hastings. I contacted the Magistrates' Association to ask about the duties of a magistrate for the WWII social history I was writing. It was almost inevitable that when Greenlit Productions asked the Magistrates' Association if they could suggest somebody who could help them with details for a WWII magistrates' court scene for the third series of Foyle's War, currently being filmed, that my name should be put forward and Greenlit rang me to ask me to be their wartime magistrates' court advisor. At first I was booked to go on location but after discussions with Greenlit they decided I would be more useful to them if I could be available to the various production departments via telephone and email, on an ad hoc basis. This went on for about three weeks. I felt disappointed that I would not meet the talented (and handsome!) actor, Michael Kitchen but he was not in the court scene anyhow. The scene was shot at St Albans because the local authority there had been circumspect in not gutting their old magistrates' court (unlike Hastings), and they now rented out the oak-panelled room to film and TV companies and for corporate and social events. I learned what minute attention to detail goes into period, TV productions: I was asked advice not just on magistrate court procedure but also on dress, hair and cosmetic styles for the female magistrate and on the deportment and language of court officials. Lady Idina Brassey, a woman mentioned by Emilie in her letters, was a magistrate in WWII Hastings and my research on Lady Idina gave me a very good idea of how a female magistrate in those times would have appeared and behaved. So you could say that the lady chairing the bench in the Foyle's War scene bears some resemblance to Lady Idina. I mentioned to the Greenlit design director that the hand-painted heraldic shields that used to hang in Hastings' old court are now displayed above the new court's stairway. Greenlit sent a photographer from their design department to meet me in Hastings and we went to the courts, where he took pictures of the shields, so that they could be reproduced for the Foyle's War court scene. The episode in which 'my' scene was set was called War of Nerves, the last episode in series three. I waited the appearance of the scene very nervously. As far as the shields were concerned it was a 'blink and you miss it' moment but every other detail seemed satisfactory to me, as I hoped it would be to the WWII-authenticity nit-pickers. I decided that I would stop being one of these henceforth; it's very difficult to get every detail right.

Working for Foyle's War in 2004 was not to be my only brush with the world of celebrity, although I wonder if Member of Parliament, Miss Ann Widdecombe would take kindly to being called a celebrity. I wrote to ask her if she would be kind enough to write a short foreword to my upcoming book about crime in WWII Hastings. I chose her in particular because of her political interest in crime and I had recently been enjoying her novels. Ann wrote the foreword to my book and later accepted my invitation to attend the launch party of Court in the Act, which was held at Hastings Town Hall, the former Magistrates' Court. Hastings Mayor, Mrs Pam Brown was the hostess and Ann was the perfect guest of honour. The 'few words' that I had asked from her were just right and she also chatted to every guest individually. Ann Widdecombe has a popularity that seems to transcend politics and her no-nonsense attitude appeals to many; I am sure Emilie Crane would have liked her. Once again the launch guests were people in my book, many of whom had lived in the Hastings area in WWII and some of them involved with upholding the law during wartime, as well as present day magistrates, police officers and councillors.

By a coincidence, Wendy Johnson was also able to attend the book launch: Some weeks previously, unaware of the date of the town hall 'do' she had arranged a flight to the UK that arrived on the morning of the launch. Weary from her early morning arrival at Heathrow, Wendy came directly to Hastings. I was very happy to welcome her and for the guests who had already read Letters from Lavender Cottage to have the opportunity to meet the lady who had made the book possible. Wendy's trip to England also included a meeting that was important to her, her family and me.

On almost every previous visit Wendy had made to London, she spent time researching her family history. At home in Canada she explored hundreds of websites where she hoped to find a lead to connect her with Emilie's and therefore her own family in England. Wendy said of her search for her relatives. "Ever since Letters from Lavender Cottage was published, Victoria and I have wondered about living descendents of Emilie Crane. We felt sure she must have some, as she mentioned many nieces and a nephew in her letters. I left several messages on genealogical websites under the name of Crane but to no avail. In July 2004 I decided to apply for a copy of Emilie's will as I felt that full names would be mentioned. When it arrived I found in it the names of Emilie's nieces, and of course Robert, her nephew, who was her executor. With his name came his address and it showed that he was an Incorporated Accountant living in Chislehurst. I started searching the internet for firms of accountants in Kent and Sussex and found one called Crane and Partners in Bromley, Kent, which is close to Chislehurst. I left an email message with a staff member at Crane and Partners and waited impatiently for a reply. It came eleven days later:

The man who contacted me was Ewart Crane, the son of Emilie's nephew, Robert. He sent me a copy of his family tree to add to the records Auntie Marion left for us, and we find that we now have dozens of new relatives. When my daughter, Heather, and I were in England in November 2004 we met the Cranes and also Emilie's niece, Olive Crane's granddaughter. It was such a happy meeting and a wonderful outcome of the search for Emilie's descendents. The internet has proven to be a faithful and fruitful companion!"

The launch of The Long Road to Lavender Cottage is planned for the spring of 2006, at a tea party in Emilie Crane's church. I anticipate with pleasure the bringing together and thanking the many generous people who have recounted to me their memories and loaned me personal photographs. To launch a book about Emilie in the church where she worshipped and where she gave her talks to the Literary Society so long ago will surely give poignancy to the event. I do not know if this will be the last book about Emilie but I do know that she will always be part of my life.

BIBLIOGRAPHY.

The Women's Movement and Women's Employment in the 19th Century. by Ellen Jordan.

A History of Helenswood School by Brian Lawes

Historic Hastings by Mainwaring Baines

Fishermen of Hastings, by Steve Peak. ISBN 0 9510706 0 6

The Second Battle of Hastings by Charles Eldridge. ISBN 0 9547279 0 8

A Short Guide for Visitors to the Ruins of the Old Parish Church of St Helen's, Ore, Sussex. By FW Bullock, son of WC Bullock Rector of Ore 1897-1929, published January 1949. Out of print.

Home - The Story of Everyone Who Ever Lived in Our House, by Julie Myerson. Published by Flamingo (2004) ISBN 0-00-714822-4

Stare Back and Smile by Joanna Lumley. Published in 1990 by Clio Press. ISBN 1-85089-424-4

The Ridge- An Ancient Highway, by Lawrence P Burgess. Sussex Life Magazine January 1971. Vol. VII Number 1

Hastings Area Archeological Research Group Journals Volume 1 No 4 July 1980 and No 1. New Series. August 1995.

Hastings Local History Group Publications.

Hastings Trolleybuses by Lyndon W Rowe. ISBN 1 873793 81 2. Published by Middleton Press. Out of print.

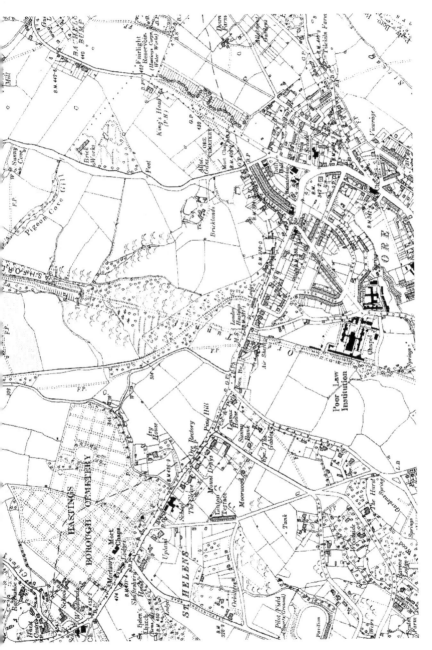

Letters from Lavender Cottage

by Victoria Seymour

Hastings in WWII and Austerity

A collection of recently discovered letters, posted from Hastings to Canada between 1942 and 1955, inspired Victoria Seymour to compile a part-biography of their writer, Emilie Crane.

In her retirement, Emilie shared a house in Hastings, England, with her two friends, Clare and Edith and their much-loved cat, James. The almost one hundred letters Emilie sent to her Canadian cousins were initially of thanks for the food parcels they had supplied to the Lavender Cottage household in WWII and throughout the following years of harsh austerity. The letters also detail the lively and kind-hearted Emilie Crane's domestic and personal life and follow the joint fortunes of the three ageing women.

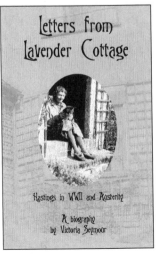

Letters from
Lavender Cottage

Hastings in WWII and Austerity

A biography
by Victoria Seymour

Victoria Seymour has rounded the story by adding contemporary national, local and autobiographical material. "Letters From Lavender Cottage" is a touching, human story with an informative narrative.

ISBN: 0-9543901-0-5   www.victoriaseymour.com

Court in the Act

written & compiled by Victoria Seymour

Crime and Policing in WWII Hastings
Foreword by Ann Widdecombe M.P.

Victoria Seymour's Court in the Act, which completes her trilogy, concentrates on the work of the police force, the magistrates' and other courts in WWII Hastings. As the effects of war took hold, there was hardly any aspect of home front life that was not controlled by some Government Act, Regulation or Order, putting even more pressure on already overworked police officers.

There passed before the courts a parade of 'spies', aliens, pacifists, looters, wartime racketeers and small-time criminals. Added to these were thousands of usually law-abiding people who found themselves in court for flouting often not properly understood laws. Sentences were handed down that sounded like something out of 19th Century history: A fine for stealing one onion from an allotment, a few apples from a tree or vegetable peelings from a dustbin or a month in prison for allowing light to escape from behind a curtain.

Meanwhile, the formidable Government Enforcers stalked the land incognito, seeking to trap unwary traders and citizens and bring them to justice. Police Court reports from the period 1939 to 1945 give an insight into a little discussed aspect of WWII. 'Vigilant', The Hastings and St Leonards Observer 1940s columnist, provides a background, with comment on the foibles and morals of a seaside town under fire.

Fact met fiction, when in 2004 Victoria Seymour was asked by Greenlit Productions, who film Foyle's War, the WWII detective television drama set in Hastings, to assist in re-creating a Hastings' wartime magistrates' court for series three.

ISBN: 0-9543901-2-1   www.victoriaseymour.com

Letters to Hannah

written & compiled by Victoria Seymour

WWII Recollections
of Hastings & South East England

Letters to Hannah looks at WWII on the Home Front through the eyes of those who lived in Hastings and South East England from September 1939 to December 1945. It also enlarges on the historical background covered in its companion book, Letters from Lavender Cottage.

Letters to Hannah visits the lives of ordinary people, who endured extraordinary times. Among many others is the account of a Battle lad, born in a cottage beside the famous 1066 battlefield. Aged fifteen he enlisted as a Home Guard, the youngest member in the country at that time, a Hastings, wartime milk delivery girl details her working and family life under fire and a young first aid volunteer highlights the horrors of bomb and machine gun attacks on civilians. 'Letters to Hannah' is rich in anecdotes and information on food rationing and shortages, the blackout, air raids, population evacuation and civil defence. The book provides a moving and factual account of wartime Hastings, the town which features in the ITV, WWII detective fiction series, Foyle's War.

Victoria Seymour links this, her second WWII social history, with a series of autobiographical letters to the future, describing her war-troubled childhood to her newborn, 21st century granddaughter, Hannah. Extracts from Letters to Hannah were included in the BBC Radio 4 history series, The Archive Hour, in July 2003.

ISBN: 0-9543901-1-3   www.victoriaseymour.com

HOST FAMILIES WANTED

Written & compiled
by Victoria Seymour

For over half century Hastings has been host to hundreds of thousands of young people from all over the world.

Host Families Wanted, the true story of overseas English language students in Hastings, is approached with the enthusiasm for detail that Victoria Seymour's regular readers expect of her.

She recounts her own experiences as student host mother, the company director of a family-run, Hastings based language school and how the work affected her life and family.

The problem of street offences against students is considered, as are the efforts of the police and the local authority to reduce the crime and protect students.

To enrich the story there are interviews with local host families and the students' teachers. In a set of essays, a group of today's overseas students comment frankly on Hastings and their hosts.

If you are a host family, have been, or are thinking of becoming one, this book is for you.

ISBN: 0-9543901-5-6
www.victoriaseymour.com